COOKING
with
COFFEE

COOKING
with
COFFEE

BREWING UP

SWEET *and* SAVORY

EVERYDAY DISHES

B R A N D I E V A N S
Creator of BranAppetit.com

Skyhorse Publishing

Visit our website at www.skyhorsepublishing.com.

10 9 8 7 6 5 4 3 2 1

Library of Congress Cataloging-in-Publication Data is available on file.

Cover design by Rain Saukas
Cover photo credit Brandi Evans

Print ISBN: 978-1-63450-223-8
Ebook ISBN: 978-1-5107-0058-1

Printed in China

For my readers and friends, thank you for all your support and encouragement along the way. And most of all, for Nick and Alden—my two best reasons for drinking even more coffee.

TABLE OF CONTENTS

SAUCES, DIPS, AND TOPPINGS

SAVORIES

SWEET & SNACKS

INTRODUCTION

My name is Brandi, and I love coffee. Of course, you're looking at a cookbook devoted completely to recipes using coffee, so I'm sure you've figured that out by now. I've been cooking up a storm and blogging/writing about what my husband and I eat for more than six years now on my blog BranAppetit (www.branappetit.com), and I'm so excited to be bringing these coffee recipes to you!

I was born and raised in Virginia and currently live in the mountains of southwest Virginia with my husband, son, Brittany Spaniel, and two cats. While we eat well now, I didn't know how to cook anything when we got married eleven years ago. After a few years of struggling in the kitchen, I decided to get serious and learn to cook. Thanks to lots of cooking shows, cookbooks, and food blogs, I slowly taught myself how to make our favorite dishes and family recipes and eventually started working on creating recipes of my own. I now create new recipes for my blog and do recipe development and testing for national brands and publications.

But you're here for the food, right? So let's get to it. I wanted this book to be more than just recipes, and that's exactly what it is! From the history of coffee to picking your brewing method and the recipes themselves, this book has it all.

Because my husband and I got serious (and a little nerdy) about our coffee methods at home, I want to pass on what we've learned throughout the past few years so you can make your best cup of coffee at home, too! We can definitely get a good cup of coffee in some shops nearby, but being able to make a perfectly brewed cup of joe in the morning is pretty nice knowledge to possess. Plus, it makes our morning routine even more enjoyable.

Coffee has been shown to have great health benefits, but most people still only use it in its most common form: brewed as a hot drink in the morning. Don't stop there, though! Coffee adds such an intense depth of flavor to other sweet and savory dishes that it should be a pantry staple for everyone. Because the roasting process and origin of the beans offer such a wide range of flavors and undertones, there's a coffee bean you can use in just about any dish. From drinks to desserts to grilled meats, coffee adds a punch to anything you're cooking.

As a self-taught cook, I try my best to make recipes and instructions simple and easy to follow. I hope you enjoy learning more about coffee and trying out some new recipes in your own kitchen!

A Brief History of the Brew

Not surprisingly, coffee is one of the most valuable traded commodities in the world. People love it! We rely on it, and, as a country, we drink it in massive quantities. It is estimated that more than two billion cups of coffee are consumed each day worldwide—each and every day!

Drinking coffee is a daily ritual in the lives of millions of humans around the globe. But where and when exactly did this habit begin?

Like most foods that have been around for hundreds of years, the origin of coffee is somewhat folkloric. According to a popular Ethiopian legend, coffee was discovered by a goat herder named Kaldi, who found his goats running around, full of energy, after eating the red berries from the coffee trees. He tried the berries for himself and had a similar reaction. After witnessing this strange behavior, a monk took some of the berries back to his fellow monks; they too spent the night awake and alert.

Before coffee became our morning beverage of choice, it was used in all kinds of preparations. In its most unprocessed form, coffee is a tiny, cherrylike fruit that becomes red when ripe. The coffee bean itself is found in the center of the red berry. Early after its discovery, the berries were mixed with fat to create protein-rich snacks. The fermented pulp was used to make winelike mixtures. Another drink that appeared around AD 1000 was made from the whole coffee fruit, including the beans and the hull. It wasn't until the thirteenth century, however, that people began to roast coffee beans, which is the first step in the process of making coffee as we know it, as a drink.

The modern version of roasted coffee began in Arabia, where, during the thirteenth century, coffee was extremely popular with the Muslim community for its ability to keep worshippers awake. The Arabians found ways of controlling the beans and their productivity, essentially cornering the market. Apparently, not a single coffee plant existed outside of Arabia or Africa until the 1600s when Baba Budan left with beans strapped across his belly. The beans he carried out of the country lead to a new and competitive European coffee trade.

In 1616, the Dutch founded the first European-owned coffee estate in Sri Lanka. The French began growing coffee in the Caribbean, followed by the Spanish in Central America and the Portuguese in Brazil. European coffeehouses popped up in Italy and France, where they gained traction. Now, in America and many other countries, it is routine to stop in a coffee shop for a cup in the morning or later for a midday pick-me-up—or both.

Although coffee plants reached the New World during the eighteenth century, coffee the drink itself wasn't really popular until the Boston Tea Party of 1773, when changing from tea to coffee became a patriotic symbol. The Civil War and other conflicts that followed also helped to increase coffee consumption, as people relied on the caffeine for energy. Teddy Roosevelt himself is counted among America's great coffee drinkers due to his (rumored) consumption of a gallon of coffee a day!

By the late 1800s, coffee had become not only a nationwide, but a world-wide commodity and people started looking for ways to profit from it. In 1864, John and Charles Arbuckle, brothers from Pittsburgh, bought Jabez Burns's newly invented coffee bean roaster. The Arbuckle brothers sold pre-roasted coffee by the pound. It wasn't long before James Folger followed and began selling coffee as well. These three men helped blazed the trail for several other big-name coffee producers, including Maxwell House and Hills Brothers. Now, of course, the country is over-run with Starbucks on every corner, Dunkin Donuts, and hundreds of local coffee shops across the world.

Benefits of Coffee

Coffee isn't just a delicious way to start your morning. Like most other whole foods, coffee boasts a variety of health benefits.

Did you know that coffee is the most widely consumed source of antioxidants in the United States? It's true! And while coffee has some great benefits, it follows the same reasoning as anything else: moderation is key. It seems that 1 to 2 cups for most people is the magic number to reap the benefits. And great news for decaf drinkers: there doesn't seem to be much difference between caffeinated drinks or decaffeinated in terms of antioxidants.

In the past few years, multiple studies on coffee and its effect in regards to many different health issues have been completed, and many more will happen, giving us an even better idea of all of the potential benefits from imbibing in a daily cup or two of delicious coffee. Some potential health benefits of drinking coffee include protecting against type 2 diabetes, Parkinson's disease, liver disease, liver cancer, and helping promote a healthy heart. The slight jolt from the caffeine can help awaken your senses and give you a boost of energy. Of course, this is also assuming you're drinking black coffee, or at least brewed coffee with maybe some milk or cream added—not the frozen coffee slushies or mostly-milk lattes.

While 1 to 2 cups, or maybe even 3 daily, fall under moderate consumption, you don't want to overdo it. Drinking too much caffeine can have adverse effects on your health and mood, essentially canceling out any potential health benefits. Indulging too much can cause mood swings, headaches, and disrupt your sleep if you have it too late in the day. As long as you're watching your overall caffeine intake, coffee can be a delicious part of your everyday routine.

Why is coffee referred to as "joe"?

One theory is that it started in the navy. Secretary of the Navy Josephus Daniels apparently banned alcohol aboard naval vessels, leaving coffee as the strongest drink on the ships. The disgruntled and now sober sailors weren't happy with the change and began referring to their coffee as a "cup of Joe."

The Roasting of the Beans

Coffee beans straight from the berries do not make a good cup of coffee. Before you can make your morning joe, the beans need to be roasted to bring out the flavor and aromatics of the different varieties of beans. While the raw beans contain all the acids and caffeine, the oils are activated by heat, which is where the flavor comes from. And while many people think that coffee is coffee is coffee, different varieties and roasting methods can bring out as many differences in coffee beans as you would find when trying to compare wines! There are subtleties, depths of flavor, hints of flowers or nuts or smoke, that are easy to pick out when you have good-quality beans and you know the right way to brew them.

Light-roasted beans are cooked for about 7 to 8 minutes, max, which is what you normally find in more of the mass-marketed coffee brands. As the roasting process suggests, these tend to be light-bodied and can often have a sour taste. They also have a dry look to them because they aren't roasted long enough for the oils in the beans to reach the surface.

Medium-roasted beans go for 9 to 11 minutes and tend to be sweeter than the light-roasted because of the extra cooking time. Medium-roasted beans also have a fuller body than the light-roasted, as well as a bit more complexity in the flavor. Medium roasts typically have dry looking beans, too, but they have a stronger flavor than the light-roasted beans.

Dark-roasted beans are exactly what you would imagine. They cook for a slightly longer amount of time, typically 12 to 13 minutes, until the acids surface. You might notice a different look of the beans compared to the light- and medium-roasted; dark-roasted beans are often shiny or oily because of the longer roasting time, where the light- and medium-roasted beans are typically dry on the outside. This roast, while it does produce the oiliest beans, also reduces the amount of acidity in the beans. Dark-roasted beans are sometimes spicy and often have a chocolaty and rich body and some sweetness or tartness.

The Essentials for Brewing

Now that you've bought your coffee beans, how are you going to make that perfect cup of joe in your own home? It's easy to get a good cup of coffee at a local shop, but making it at home does take a little practice and know-how. Luckily, it won't take much time to figure out how to make your perfect cup of coffee!

The most important step is finding the coffee beans (origin, roast, flavors) that you like. My husband and I are hooked on coffee from Lexington Roasters in Lexington, Virginia, and we tend to favor the fruitier beans, with a tarter aftertaste than one that may be more smoky or chocolaty. You may simply need to buy a few different varieties to see which ones you like the best.

The origin of your coffee beans dictates the flavors and subtleties that will come through in the brewing process, regardless of how it was roasted. Each location produces coffee beans that have unique qualities. The soil, weather, and environment of specific regions affect both the growing conditions of the plants and the flavor of the beans themselves. Beans from Africa and Arabia tend to have sweet undertones with fruity and tart aromas and are fairly acidic. Coffee from the Americas (Caribbean, Mexico, Central and South America) are often light- or medium-bodied and slightly sweet. These are usually well balanced and are often used in coffee blends for that reason. Coffee from Asia, Indonesia, and the Pacific regions are on the opposite end of the spectrum: full-bodied, low acidity, smooth. These often have a more earthy, sometimes smoky, or chocolatey aroma.

Picking the right coffee really just comes down to taking the time to sample different origins, different roasts, and different brewing methods. But once you know whether you love a fruitier, more tart coffee or a smoky, rich, earthy coffee, you're on your way to brewing the perfect cup at home.

Once you have your coffee at home, it's time to decide how you want to brew it for your morning cup. The amount of time you have in the morning may determine which method you choose; however, no matter which method you like the best, you can always try new ones or switch up your routine on the weekends when you might have more time to spend on breakfast and coffee.

Regardless of whether you use your good old countertop coffeepot or a pour-over brewing system, the most important thing is that you start out with good beans and a good attitude. You're about to make great coffee, but what exactly do you need?

- Good, whole coffee beans, stored in an airtight container (*not* in the refrigerator or freezer)
- A coffee grinder with at least 3 to 4 different settings*
- Clean brewing equipment, depending on what you plan to use (automatic, french press, etc.)
- Kitchen scale to weigh out beans
- Filtered/spring water for brewing

*Note: After trying a few different options, my husband and I fell in love with the Capresso Infinity Burr Grinder, and we use it every day. It has a variety of settings for different grinds depending on your brewing preference and it is easy to use and clean. If you know you'll only make coffee one way at home (either in a drip machine or french press or pour-over exclusively), you can get a single-setting grinder for what you need and spend a little less money. If you think you might be brewing your coffee a few different ways at home, you may want to have a grinder with setting options.

Coffee in the pantry, fridge, or freezer?

If you're stashing your coffee in the freezer, you're not the only one. We used to do the same thing!

The great news is that if you're a daily coffee drinker, there's no need to keep it in the fridge or freezer. In fact, storing it in either of those places can create moisture, and too much moisture will ruin your beans. The humid environment, plus the daily removing and replacing, will cause your coffee to lose all of its subtleties and flavor and can actually cause the beans to simply go bad before you may finish the bag.

If you buy beans in bulk, you can store them in the freezer until you're ready to open a bag. Then simply keep your current/open bag or container of beans in an airtight container on your counter or in your pantry.

How to Brew—Different Methods

While everyone likes their coffee a little different, these instructions for different brewing methods are the best place to start. You may still need to adjust either amounts of coffee or brewing time, depending on your personal preference—and those adjustments are completely worth it!

Automatic Coffeemaker

While many people now scoff at the typical countertop coffeepot, you can still make a great cup of coffee using this machine. One of the biggest mistakes we used to make when using our automatic coffeemaker was simply that we didn't use enough beans. We were measuring based on typical instructions, but if you like your coffee strong, you may need to use quite a bit more when brewing a pot. It does take longer to brew an entire pot of coffee in an automatic maker compared to doing a pour-over or french press, for example, which does affect the coffee, but if this is your only option, you can still make a great pot of coffee!

- I will always suggest using spring water to brew coffee, especially if you have hard water or other issues, just to ensure that the only flavor in your coffee is coming from the beans themselves.
- For an average 12-cup automatic coffeemaker, we use 50 grams of coffee beans, which measures out to just over 4 grams per cup. Since the grounds sit in the filter in the coffeemaker, there's not much of a chance that any will end up the pot (unless something goes wrong), so we typically grind them on a medium setting.
- Compared to other methods, we use the least amount of beans when brewing in an automatic coffeemaker because it does take longer to brew, so the grounds have more time to give off their oils and flavor.

French Press

The french press, or press pot, is one of the easiest ways to brew at home while giving you more control over the brewing process. You don't need much besides the french press itself, but you will need a timer!

- For an 8-cup french press, weigh out 56 grams of coffee beans and grind on a fairly coarse setting. Since you'll be pouring the coffee through the filter on the french press, you want the grounds fairly large to make sure they don't end up in the bottom of your cup.
- Pour the ground coffee into the bottom of the french press.
- Bring water to a boil on the stovetop. Once it has begun to boil, remove it from the heat and let it sit for at least 30 seconds (you want it around 200 to 205 degrees Fahrenheit).

- Pour the hot water over the coffee in the french press, making sure to get all the grounds saturated.
- Set the timer for 1 minute. Stir the bloom (the top layer) and place the lid on the french press, but do not press down yet.
- Set your timer for 4 minutes. Once the timer goes off, press down and serve immediately. If you won't be drinking the entire french press pot at one time, at least pour it into a travel mug or other vessel so the coffee doesn't sit any longer with the grounds.

Pour-Over

The pour-over method is one that has become quite popular lately and can be found as an option on many coffeehouse menus. At the most basic level, the pour-over serves as a filter basket that sits right over your coffee mug. We like using the pour-over method at home, especially on weekday mornings, because we can make just one cup of coffee at a time and it doesn't take long to do.

The grind will be different for pour-over compared to french press because we want the water to easily brew through the grinds and get the most amount of flavor possible without worrying whether the grounds will end up in our cup (they won't).

- For about a 10-ounce cup, weigh out 20 grams of coffee beans. Grind them on a fine setting, similar to the size of salt granules.

- Place a #4 (fits most pour-over containers) filter into your dripper and run some hot water over the filter to get it wet. Empty any extra water out of the dripper.
- Pour the ground coffee into the bottom of the pour-over filter.
- Bring water to a boil on the stovetop. Once it begins to boil, remove it from the heat and let it sit for at least 30 seconds (you want it around 200 to 205 degrees Fahrenheit).
- If you have a pour-over without a stopper, you want to make sure you have yours sitting on your coffee mug before adding the water.
- If you have a pour-over with a stopper, keep it on the counter to let it brew, and place it on your mug to dispense the coffee once the brewing is complete.

- Pour just enough of the hot water over the coffee to soak all the grounds, then stop and let the mixture bloom for 30 seconds.
- Continue pouring water over the coffee, swirling to get the sides until you've reached the top of the dripper.
  - If using a no-stopper pour-over, let the coffee drip into your mug until full and the drips have slowed.
  - If you're using a pour-over with a stopper, set your timer for 3 minutes. Once the timer goes off, place the pour-over on your coffee mug to release the coffee.
- Discard the filter and clean the pour-over before your next use.

Siphon

A siphon, or vacuum pot, is a little more time-consuming than other brewing methods, but I think it's also the most fun! It makes your kitchen feel like a science lab and can be a great conversation-starter if you have houseguests.

The vacuum pot brews coffee by using two chambers where vapor pressure and vacuum produces the coffee. They have been used to make coffee now for more than a century.

During this process, you use the heating and cooling of the pot to change the vapor pressure and force the water up, brewing the coffee, and then releasing the liquid back into the lower chamber once the heat and pressure lowers. This leaves your brewed coffee in the bottom carafe or chamber and the used coffee grounds in the top chamber. Yeah, science!

- For a 20-ounce siphon or vacuum pot, weigh out 40 grams of coffee beans (about 6 tablespoons). If your siphon is a different size, adjust accordingly.
- Grind the beans fine, about the size of table salt.
- Fill the bottom chamber with 20 ounces of water.
- Pour the grounds into the top chamber and place it on top of the water chamber.
- Bring the water to a boil and then lower the heat to medium to keep it at a slow simmer.

- The hot water will start rising into the top chamber. Once all the water is in with the coffee, give the mixture a stir to make sure all the coffee is saturated.
- Set your timer for 3 minutes and 30 seconds. Once there's about 1 minute left, remove the siphon from the heat and set it on a hot pad.
- The brewed coffee will drain back into the bottom chamber, leaving the grounds in the top. Once all the coffee is in the bottom chamber, remove the top, discard the grounds, and serve.

Chemex

The Chemex is a self-contained pour-over container that works almost the same exact way as a single cup pour-over setup, but you can make multiple cups at a time. Also, once the brewing process is done, the coffee is already in a carafe, ready to serve! Perfect for entertaining and a beautiful way to serve coffee in the morning or with dessert.

- For about a typical 40-ounce Chemex, weigh out 42 grams of coffee (about 6 table-spoons). Grind them somewhat coarsely, about the size of kosher salt.
- Place the Chemex filter inside, with the folds lining up with the spout.
- Wet the filter with hot water, then pour out the water.
- Pour the ground coffee into the filter.
- Bring water to a boil on the stovetop. Once it has begun to boil, remove it from the heat and let it sit for at least 30 seconds (you want it around 200 to 205 degrees Fahrenheit).
- Pour just enough of the hot water over the coffee to soak all the grounds, then stop and let the mixture bloom for 30 seconds.
- Continue pouring water over the coffee, swirling to get the sides, until you've reached the top of the filter.
- Continue to add hot water until the coffee reaches the glass button on the Chemex.
- Remove the filter from the Chemex and serve.

There are a few more brewing methods you can try, but these are the easiest to do at home and they make some of the best cups of coffee you'll ever have!

Popular Ingredients to Use with Coffee

Now that you've found your favorite coffee beans, you're ready to get cooking! But what works well with coffee in recipes? I honestly haven't found much that doesn't go well with a little bit of coffee, but there are definitely ingredients that pair really well with coffee and should always be put together when possible.

For sweet recipes, chocolate is probably the most popular and easiest to work with. Chocolate and coffee can be put together in just about anything and be great. They play off each other and balance each other out, while bringing out the best characteristics of both. Whether you're making a chocolate cake or icing or brownies or cookies, it's a sure bet that mixing chocolate and coffee together is a good idea.

I also love using vanilla and brown sugar with coffee. The rich flavors pair well with coffee, regardless of whether you're using a fruitier, more tart coffee or a smoky, earthy bean. If you're using a fruity, tart coffee bean, berries of all kinds are also a great choice, whether to simply serve along with a good cup of coffee or for baking (maybe a raspberry coffee scone?).

When you want to make a savory recipe with coffee—grilled meat or a sauce or stew—the most important part is to be aware of the flavor in the coffee you're using (fruity, tart, smoky, earthy, etc.) and make sure anything else you use helps to balance it out, especially if your coffee has any bitterness to it. Say, for instance, you want to make a salad dressing using some coffee. Either a fruitier or smoky coffee would work well, but you want to make sure you add in a little sweetener (I like pure maple syrup or honey) to help balance it out, plus a little of your favorite vinegar and oil to bring out the richness and a little zing to the dressing.

My favorite savory ingredients to use with coffee are definitely any kind of pepper or chile (the smokiness and heat of the peppers pairs perfectly with coffee), tomatoes, smoky spices like paprika or chili powders, and any kind of meat.

Anything that tastes good roasted is also usually a safe bet to pair with coffee, so nuts or root vegetables are a great way to expand your coffee cooking experiments.

Potatoes are especially good with coffee, as are most carb-y items. Honestly, all you have to do is dust some ground coffee over a steak with a little salt, pepper, and oil and you'll have a delicious meal. It doesn't have to be complicated to be good!

Cooking and Baking with Coffee

Of course, cooking and baking with coffee is different than just brewing a cup to drink in the morning. But once you have some set flavor pairings down, it's easy (and fun!) to start adding coffee to your favorite recipes and see how they turn out.

As with most things, it's much easier to add in new ingredients or swap things out when you're cooking versus baking. Cooking can be much more intuitive and spontaneous, while baking is more of a science. For anything you're cooking or mixing up to use for a savory dish, I say go for it! Try whatever you think sounds good, and see how it works. Sometimes it won't, and that's okay. You'll know for next time. For marinades and dressings and sauces, you really can't go wrong. The best part about using coffee in savory recipes (or at least non-baked goods) is that you can taste as you go and adjust as needed.

With baking, it's a bit different. Because everything in baking needs to be measured and accurate, it is a little tougher to simply toss in some coffee. However, it's possible! If you want to use brewed coffee in a recipe, I'd start with replacing one third to one half of the liquid in the recipe with brewed, cooled coffee and see how it turns out. If you'd rather not deal with that, you can always add in some finely ground coffee beans or instant espresso. Since those add a big punch of flavor without much volume, you typically don't have to adjust any other ingredients, but you still end up with great coffee flavor in the finished product.

For recipes that require a really intense coffee flavor, I would suggest using multiple coffee sources—brewed and ground or even whole, cracked beans in the finished dish or as a garnish. It's also nice to use ground coffee beans or instant espresso in dishes so you can see the little specks of coffee, like in spiced whipped cream or scones or a glaze.

All the recipes in this cookbook have been tested and approved by myself and my husband, so these are a great place to start cooking with coffee. I also hope you find new ways to use it in both sweet and savory dishes and experiment on your own!

BREAKFAST

Ah, breakfast. It has always been my favorite meal of the day, regardless of whether I'm having it in the morning or making breakfast for dinner. Either way, there's something special about breakfast foods and the comfort inherent in every dish. We loved trying all these recipes, and hope you love them, too!

Multigrain Waffles with Vanilla Maple Glaze

Makes 6–8 servings

I couldn't have a breakfast section in this book without having a waffle recipe. If there's one single-use kitchen appliance you buy, I would definitely suggest getting a good-quality waffle iron. It really makes a difference! These waffles, even with half whole-wheat flour, are light and crispy thanks to the seltzer. They're best eaten hot, right off the iron, but you can also stash them in a 250°F oven as you cook to keep them warm and crisp.

Waffles
1 cup all-purpose flour
1 cup whole-wheat pastry flour
1 tablespoon sugar
½ teaspoon baking soda
¼ teaspoon salt
2 eggs

½ cup yogurt
¼ cup buttermilk
½ teaspoon vanilla extract
¼ cup safflower or vegetable oil
1 cup seltzer water

In a large bowl, mix the all-purpose flour, whole-wheat pastry flour, sugar, baking soda, and salt together. Beat the eggs, then add to the dry ingredients, along with the yogurt, buttermilk, vanilla extract, and oil. Stir in the seltzer.

On a large, round waffle iron, drop about ½ cup of batter for each waffle and cook until crisp and golden. While the remaining waffles are cooking, keep the finished waffles warm in the oven (this will help keep them crispy).

Serve the waffles warm with some of the Vanilla Maple Glaze (page 84) and softened butter.

Coffee Shop Muffins

Makes 6 muffins

Technically, these are muffins. In spirit, they're a cross between a muffin and a classic cake donut, covered in some melted butter and cinnamon sugar. The nutmeg pairs so well with the coffee flavor, and the cinnamon sugar topping adds a little something special.

2 tablespoons softened butter
2 tablespoons safflower or vegetable oil
¼ cup sugar
3 tablespoons brown sugar
1 egg
1 teaspoon instant espresso
1 teaspoon baking powder
⅛ teaspoon baking soda
¾ teaspoon ground nutmeg
½ teaspoon salt

1 teaspoon vanilla extract
1⅓ cups all-purpose flour
¼ cup milk
¼ cup coffee, cooled

For rolling after baking
2 tablespoons butter, melted
2 tablespoons sugar
2 teaspoons cinnamon

Grease your muffin tray or place liners in 6 of the spaces.

Preheat oven to 425°F.

Cream the butter, oil, and sugars together. Add in the egg and mix thoroughly.

Stir in the instant espresso, baking powder, baking soda, nutmeg, salt, and vanilla.

Gently stir in half of the flour, then half of both the milk and coffee. Add the remaining flour and the rest of the milk and coffee.

Fill 6 spaces in the muffin tray and bake for 15–17 minutes or until set and a toothpick comes out clean.

Let the muffins cool about 5 minutes. Dip the tops of the muffins in the melted butter and then roll them through the sugar and cinnamon.

Coffee Vanilla Banana Bread

Makes 2 loaves

I love a good, classic banana bread and this one fits the bill. With the addition of instant espresso, it becomes the perfect slice to have for breakfast or as an afternoon snack. Feel free to add in your favorite spices, nuts, chocolate chips, or other mix-ins!

2 cups bananas, mashed
½ cup butter, melted
1 cup sugar
3 eggs, beaten
2½ cups flour

1 teaspoon salt
1 teaspoon baking soda
1 teaspoon vanilla extract
2 tablespoons instant espresso
1 cup nuts, chopped

Preheat oven to 350°F.

Mix the bananas with the butter, sugar, and eggs.

Stir in the flour, salt, baking soda, vanilla, espresso, and nuts.

Grease two loaf pans (either 8½" x 4½" or 9" x 5") and divide the batter between the two pans.

Bake for 60–70 minutes or until a toothpick comes out clean.

Makes 8 servings

Is there anything better than a hot, doughy cinnamon roll, right out of the oven? Well, one thing can make them better: a rich, sweet, coffee glaze drizzled all over the top. These are perfect for a fun weekend breakfast or serving overnight guests.

1 tablespoon active dry yeast
1¼ cups milk, warmed to just above room
    temperature
2 tablespoons butter, melted
2 tablespoons sugar
½ teaspoon salt
3 cups all-purpose flour
1 cup whole-wheat flour
2 eggs
4 tablespoons butter, softened
1 tablespoon instant espresso

2 teaspoons cinnamon
½ teaspoon ground nutmeg
⅓ cup sugar

Coffee Glaze
1½ cups powdered sugar
1 tablespoon pure maple syrup
2 tablespoons brewed, chilled coffee
½ teaspoon vanilla bean paste
1–2 tablespoons milk, to thin glaze

In the bowl of a stand mixer (or other large bowl), mix the yeast with the warmed milk. Let this mixture sit about 5 minutes until the yeast is foamy.

Add the butter, 2 tablespoons sugar, salt, flours, and eggs, and mix 5–10 minutes with a dough hook (or your hands) until everything is combined and the dough is smooth.

Put the dough in an oiled bowl and let it rise, covered, in a warm place until doubled (about 1 hour).

Punch down the dough and roll out into a large rectangle, about 10 x 14, on a floured surface.

Spread the softened butter on the dough with your hands and sprinkle on the instant espresso, cinnamon, nutmeg, and sugar.

Starting with one of the long sides, roll up the dough and pinch the seam sealed with your fingertips.

Slice the dough into 1-inch thick pieces and place them on a greased baking dish.

Cover the rolls and let them rise again, until puffed and almost doubled, about 30 minutes to 1 hour.

In the meantime, heat oven to 350°F.

Bake the rolls 20–25 minutes until golden on the edges. Let them cool at least 10–15 minutes before adding the glaze (the longer you wait, the better the glaze will do).

In a medium bowl, mix the powdered sugar with the maple syrup, coffee, and vanilla bean paste. Add 1–2 tablespoons (or more) of milk until the glaze is as thick as you'd like.

Spread the glaze on the rolls before serving.

Mocha Chip Baked Oatmeal

Makes 6 servings

One of the first hot breakfasts I fell in love with was oatmeal, and I love finding new ways to use it. The main reason I love this dish is that you can mix it up right in the baking dish—no need to dirty another bowl! Plus you can customize this with anything you have on hand—dried fruits, nuts, spices. Have fun with it!

½ cup milk
½ cup brewed coffee, cooled
1 teaspoon vanilla extract
½ teaspoon salt
½ cup unsweetened applesauce
2 eggs, beaten
1½ teaspoons baking powder
2 cups oats
¾ cup chocolate chips

Preheat oven to 350°F.

Grease an 8 x 8 baking dish.

Pour the milk, coffee, vanilla, salt, and applesauce into the pan. Mix in the beaten eggs.

Gently stir in the baking powder, oats, and chocolate chips.

Bake for 35–40 minutes.

Espresso Banana Muffins

Makes 12 muffins

Muffins are such a great quick breakfast or snack, and espresso and banana together make for a delicious combination. These would be perfect to make on the weekend to have as an easy grab-and-go choice during your busy week. I like mine split in half, toasted a little bit, and topped with butter, but jam is also incredible on these muffins!

2 cups bananas (about 3 medium bananas), mashed
½ cup butter, melted
¾ cup sugar
2 eggs, beaten
1 teaspoon vanilla extract
1 tablespoon instant espresso
2 cups flour
1 teaspoon salt
1 teaspoon baking soda
1 cup walnuts, chopped

Preheat the oven to 350°F.

Mix the bananas with the butter, sugar, beaten eggs, and vanilla.

Stir in the instant espresso, flour, salt, baking soda, and chopped walnuts.

Fill the muffin tin and bake for 25–30 minutes or until a toothpick comes out clean.

Mocha Coconut Almond Granola

Makes 6 cups granola

I feel like granola often gets overlooked. While some varieties can be pretty high in calories, you can customize it to fit exactly what you want. Plus, most of the ingredients in granola are healthy, whole foods—oats, grains, nuts, seeds—so it's a great choice to have with milk or yogurt in the morning. This mix uses coffee and cocoa powder for a mocha flavor and is tossed with coconut and mini chocolate chips for a little indulgence.

4 cups old-fashioned oats
1 cup almonds, slivered
2 tablespoons water
½ cup pure maple syrup
2 tablespoons oil (light oil like safflower or melted coconut oil)

2 tablespoons unsweetened cocoa powder
3 tablespoons brewed, chilled coffee
1 teaspoon vanilla extract
½ teaspoon salt
½ cup mini chocolate chips
½ cup unsweetened coconut flakes

Preheat oven to 275°F.

Mix the oats and almonds together in a large bowl.

In a saucepan over medium heat, mix the water, maple syrup, oil, cocoa, coffee, vanilla extract, and salt until the cocoa is dissolved.

Pour the mixture over the oats and almonds and stir everything together.

Spread the oat mixture on a parchment-lined baking sheet and bake for 20 minutes. Remove from the oven and stir. Bake another 20–30 minutes until the granola is mostly dry.

Let it cool completely. Stir to break up the granola and add in the chocolate chips and coconut.

Coffee and White Chocolate Chip Coffee Cake

Makes 12 servings

Growing up, I always thought coffee cake was made with coffee. Turns out, most recipes don't include it in the ingredients! Since I love the flavor of coffee—especially in baked goods, and alongside a cup of coffee—I came up with a coffee cake that uses instant espresso for a punch of coffee flavor and white chocolate chips for some sweetness.

Cake
1 cup buttermilk
⅓ cup vegetable or safflower oil
⅓ cup sugar
1½ tablespoons instant espresso
1 teaspoon vanilla extract
¾ cup all-purpose flour
¾ cup white whole-wheat flour
2 teaspoons baking powder
½ teaspoon salt
¾ cup white chocolate chips

Streusel
½ cup all-purpose flour
⅓ cup brown sugar, packed
¼ cup granulated sugar
¼ cup quick oats
4 tablespoons butter, melted

Preheat oven to 375°F.

In a medium bowl, mix the buttermilk, oil, sugar, espresso, and vanilla together. Stir in the flours, baking powder, and salt. Fold in the white chocolate chips. Pour batter into an 8 x 8 baking dish.

In a small bowl, mix the flour, brown sugar, granulated sugar, oats, and melted butter together. Sprinkle the streusel topping over the top of the batter.

Bake 35–40 minutes or until a toothpick comes out clean.

Orange Mocha Chip Scones

Makes 10–12 scones

Over the past few years, scones have become one of my favorite things to bake at home. Once you get the basic dough recipe down, they'll turn into one of your favorite things, too. The best part about these scones is that you don't have to cut butter into the flour, which means less work and *one less ingredient!*

2 cups all-purpose flour
1½ tablespoons baking powder
2 tablespoons fresh orange zest
1 tablespoon sugar
1 tablespoon instant espresso

½ teaspoon salt
1 cup dark chocolate chips
1½ cups heavy cream, plus 2 tablespoons for
    brushing the tops of the scones
1 egg, beaten

Preheat oven to 425°. Line a baking sheet with parchment paper or get out a baking stone.

In a large bowl, mix the flour, baking powder, orange zest, sugar, instant espresso, salt, and chocolate chips.

Mix the 1½ cups heavy cream with the beaten egg and stir the cream mixture into the dry ingredients. The dough needs to come together and will still be a little sticky. If there are still dry patches of flour, gently work them in.

Dump the dough onto a floured pastry cloth or floured surface.

Mound the dough into one piece, gently, and pat out until it's about ¾-inch thick.

Cut out triangles or rounds, using a biscuit cutter or knife, and place on stone or tray. Gather the scraps of dough, gently put them back together, and pat out again, cutting scones until you're out of dough.

Brush the tops of the scones with heavy cream.

Bake for 12–15 minutes until golden around the edges.

Salted Coffee Ricotta Toast

Makes 2 servings

I know what you might be thinking: ricotta on toast for breakfast? Don't knock it until you try it! My husband and I had something similar at a little café in Montreal and I couldn't stop thinking about it once we got home. This mix, with the coffee and vanilla, almost tastes like a cannoli filling on your morning toast.

1 cup whole milk ricotta cheese
1 tablespoon instant espresso
1–2 tablespoons brewed coffee, cooled
½ teaspoon vanilla extract
4 slices bread, toasted and buttered
2 tablespoons honey
½ teaspoon large flake sea salt

Mix the ricotta cheese with the instant espresso, brewed coffee, and vanilla extract.

Spread the ricotta on the toasted bread and top with honey and sea salt.

Espresso Vanilla Chip Scones with Vanilla Espresso Glaze

Makes 10–12 scones

Already in love with the orange scones in the book? Then you'll love this version! It's almost the same exact dough base (easy and only one bowl needed) with a simple vanilla espresso glaze to drizzle over the top. Want to impress visitors or bring something fancy but easy to a brunch? Whip up a batch of these and watch them disappear.

2 cups all-purpose flour
1½ tablespoons baking powder
1 tablespoon sugar
1 tablespoon instant espresso
½ teaspoon salt
1 cup dark chocolate chips
1½ cups heavy cream, plus 2 tablespoons for brushing the tops of the scones
1 egg, beaten
1 teaspoon vanilla bean paste

Vanilla Espresso Glaze
1 cup powdered sugar
½ teaspoon instant espresso
½ teaspoon vanilla bean paste or vanilla extract
1 tablespoon brewed coffee, cooled
1 tablespoon milk

Preheat oven to 425°F. Line a baking sheet with parchment paper or get out a baking stone.

In a large bowl, mix the flour, baking powder, orange zest, sugar, instant espresso, salt, and chocolate chips.

Mix the 1½ cups heavy cream with the beaten egg and vanilla bean paste, and stir the cream mixture into the dry ingredients. The dough needs to come together and will still be a little sticky. If there are still dry patches of flour, gently work them in.

Dump the dough onto a floured pastry cloth or floured surface.

Mound the dough into one piece, gently, and pat out until it's about ¾-inch thick.

Continued on following page.

Cut out triangles or rounds, using a biscuit cutter or knife, and place on stone or tray. Gather the scraps of dough, gently put them back together, and pat out again, cutting scones until you're out of dough.

Brush the tops of the scones with heavy cream.

Bake for 12–15 minutes until golden around the edges.

In a medium bowl, mix the powdered sugar with the instant espresso and vanilla bean paste. Add the coffee and milk and stir until the mixture is smooth. If the glaze is too thick, add a bit more liquid.

Spread the glaze on the scones once they have cooled completely.

HOMEMADE COFFEE CREAMERS

If you're a fan of cream in your coffee, I can't wait for you to try these homemade creamers! My husband is a coffee purist (a.k.a., drinks it black—and only black), but I like a little splash of milk or cream in mine. And while I normally stick with milk or cream, I do like having a little flavor in my coffee every now and then. But I don't like all the ingredients in store-bought creamers, so I've come up with some great flavors you can make at home. I'm also not a big fan of overly sweet coffee drinks, so these creamers are just sweet enough for me. Feel free to adjust the sweeteners to get it just how you like it!

Salted Chocolate

Makes 2 cups creamer

I don't know about you, but I like a salt with my chocolate—even in coffee! There's just enough salt to balance out the sweetness of the chocolate creamer, and it's especially delicious in iced coffee!

4 tablespoons pure maple syrup or sugar
2 tablespoons unsweetened cocoa powder
1 teaspoon water
½ teaspoon vanilla extract
1⅓ cups heavy cream
⅔ cup whole milk
½–1 teaspoon salt (to taste)

In a pot over medium heat, mix the maple syrup, cocoa powder, water, and vanilla extract together until the cocoa is incorporated into the liquids.

Once the mixture is smooth, pour in the cream and milk, and let it heat until bubbles begin to form around the edges.

Remove the pan from heat and stir in the salt. Pour into a container and chill before serving.

Note: This creamer may separate a bit in the fridge as it cools, with the chocolaty layer settling near the bottom. Just give it a good shake or stir before pouring into your cup.

Spiced Chocolate

Makes 1 cup creamer

If you've ever had a Mexican-spiced coffee drink or candy, you'll probably recognize most of these spices together. I know how strange it sounds to have black pepper and/or cayenne in a coffee creamer, but it's the perfect amount of punch with the sweet honey, cinnamon, and cocoa powder. Definitely taste as you go to make sure you don't get it too spicy!

½ cup cream
½ cup milk
2 tablespoons honey
1 tablespoon unsweetened cocoa powder
1 teaspoon cinnamon
½ teaspoon vanilla extract
¼ teaspoon salt
⅛ teaspoon black pepper
pinch cayenne (to taste)

In a pot over medium heat, mix the cream, milk, honey, cocoa powder, cinnamon, vanilla extract, salt, black pepper, and cayenne together until the cocoa is incorporated into the liquids.

Bring the mixture to a low simmer, just until bubbles begin to form around the edge of the pan.

Remove the pan from heat and let it cool for 5–10 minutes. Pour into an airtight container and cool in the refrigerator.

Note: This creamer may separate a bit in the fridge as it cools with the chocolaty layer settling near the bottom. Just give it a good shake or stir before pouring into your cup.

Coconut Almond

Makes about 1 cup creamer

Sometimes you feel like a nut . . . sometimes you don't. This homemade creamer has all the familiar flavors of a classic coconut-almond candy, but with a bit less sugar. If you like your coconut and cocoa without almonds, or would rather use pecans or walnuts or even hazelnuts, swap the almonds out for your favorite!

½ cup heavy cream
½ cup milk
1 tablespoon unsweetened cocoa powder
1 tablespoon unsweetened coconut flakes
1 tablespoon almonds, slivered
1 tablespoon honey or maple syrup
¼ teaspoon salt

In a pot over medium heat, mix the cream, milk, cocoa powder, coconut, almonds, honey or maple syrup, and salt together until the cocoa is incorporated into the liquids.

Bring the mixture to a low simmer, just until bubbles begin to form around the edge of the pan.

Remove the pan from heat and let it cool for 5–10 minutes. Pour into an airtight container and cool in the refrigerator.

Note: This creamer may separate a bit in the fridge as it cools with the chocolaty layer settling near the bottom. Just give it a good shake or stir before pouring into your cup.

Vanilla Bean

Makes 2 cups creamer

If you love having cream in your coffee, but aren't a big fan of other flavors (cocoa, almond, coconut, etc), this is the perfect cream for you! Just a hint of vanilla and maple syrup adds just enough sweetness to your morning cup. This is also delicious in hot tea!

1⅓ cups heavy cream
⅔ cup whole milk
4 tablespoons pure maple syrup
½ teaspoon vanilla bean paste

Heat the cream, milk, and maple syrup together in microwave-safe bowl or over medium heat on stovetop until bubbles form around the edges and the maple syrup dissolves into the cream and milk.

Stir in the vanilla bean paste.

Pour into a container and let it cool before serving.

Pumpkin Spice

Makes 1 cup of creamer

Ah, pumpkin spice coffee. It seems that most people either absolutely love it or cannot stand it. If you're on the love side—or are looking for a healthier option to make yourself—I've got you covered. This creamer uses real pumpkin, not just spices, for the flavor. Plus, compared to store-bought options, you can pronounce (and more than likely already have) all the ingredients.

½ cup heavy cream
½ cup whole milk
2 tablespoons maple syrup
2 tablespoons pumpkin purée
½ teaspoon cinnamon
¼ teaspoon ground ginger
pinch nutmeg
pinch salt

Mix the cream, milk, maple syrup, pumpkin purée, cinnamon, ginger, nutmeg, and salt together in a medium saucepan.

Bring the mixture to a low simmer and cook, stirring occasionally, for 5 minutes.

Strain the mixture through a fine sieve and store in the fridge.

German Chocolate

Makes 1 cup creamer

If you could stir a slice of cake into your coffee, wouldn't you? I know I'd like to do that some days. This is probably my favorite of the creamer recipes, simply because it takes all the best things from my favorite German chocolate cake and infuses them into cream for my morning cup of coffee. This one also works great in iced coffee for a little extra flavor!

½ cup cream
½ cup milk
1 tablespoon maple syrup
1 tablespoon unsweetened cocoa powder
1 tablespoon unsweetened shredded coconut
1 tablespoon pecans
¼ teaspoon salt

Mix the cream, milk, maple syrup, cocoa powder, coconut, pecans, and salt together in a medium saucepan.

Bring the mixture to a low simmer and cook, stirring occasionally, for 5 minutes.

Strain the mixture through a fine sieve and store in the fridge.

Cinnamon Pecan

Makes 1 cup creamer

Cinnamon and pecans are meant to be together, whether in sticky buns, oatmeal, or coffee creamer. The warm cinnamon pairs so well with the sweet pecans, making this a great option to have on hand in the morning for you or for guests.

½ cup heavy cream
½ cup whole milk
1 tablespoon honey
1 tablespoon pecans
1 teaspoon cinnamon
¼ teaspoon salt

Mix the cream, milk, honey, pecans, cinnamon, and salt together in a medium saucepan.

Bring the mixture to a low simmer and cook, stirring occasionally, for 5 minutes.

Strain the mixture through a fine sieve and store in the fridge.

DRINKS & SMOOTHIES

Most coffee drink recipes you'll find are for frozen slushy type treats, but you can do so much more! I love a good frozen mocha as much as the next person, but don't let yourself get into a smoothie rut. If you've got some extra coffee, you're ready to make any of these drinks or smoothies at home. Bonus — did you know you could make your own Irish Cream? It's one of my new favorite things and is now one of the most requested items from my family.

Cold Brew Coffee Concentrate

Makes 3-4 servings

I'll admit it: I was late to the cold brew coffee/iced coffee trend. Until I had a glass of really well-made iced coffee, I thought it was gross. But if you start with good coffee, and brew it the right way, cold brew coffee will probably become one of your favorite drinks, too. Especially on a hot summer morning. I really like making a big batch of cold brew decaf to have as an afternoon treat on summer days.

⅔ cup coffee beans
3 cups filtered water
milk or cream, to taste

Grind the beans on a fairly coarse setting, similar to what you would use for a french press. If you grind them too fine, grinds may end up in your finished cup of coffee.

Pour the ground coffee into a 4-cup french press or pitcher (or Toddy cold brew system) and slowly add the water. Gently stir the water and coffee together to make sure there are no dry spots of beans.

Place in the refrigerator and let it sit at least 8 hours.

After 8 hours (or longer, if you'd like), drain the coffee out into a separate container either using your french press to separate the coffee grounds or pouring through a few layers of cheesecloth or coffee filters. Discard the grounds.

Serve chilled, on ice, with milk or cream to taste.

Makes 2 servings

Vanilla and coffee is always a good combination. I love how simple this smoothie is, and how easy it is to whip up in the mornings. For busy days or a quick afternoon snack, this vanilla bean smoothie is a great way to use up a little extra coffee.

5 ounces vanilla yogurt
½ cup brewed coffee, cooled
½ cup milk
½ teaspoon vanilla bean paste or vanilla extract
1 cup ice

Add all ingredients to a blender and process until all the ice is broken up and the mixture is smooth. Serve immediately.

Mocha Freeze

Makes 2 servings

As a self-professed chocoholic, I will almost always choose chocolate over vanilla. And this is no exception. Take the basic vanilla smoothie, add a little cocoa powder, and you're set! No fancy syrups needed, and it definitely costs less than five dollars to make at home.

5 ounces yogurt (plain, vanilla, or chocolate)
½ cup brewed coffee, cooled
½ cup milk
½ teaspoon vanilla
1½ tablespoons unsweetened cocoa powder
1 cup ice

Add all ingredients to a blender and process until the ice is broken up and the mixture is smooth. Serve immediately.

Strawberry Chocolate Chiller

Makes 2 servings

Any time I make a smoothie, I try to find ways to add more fruits and/or vegetables to the mix. It's a great way to sneak in some extra nutrition, and fruits and vegetables add fantastic flavor and texture to the smoothie, as well. I like using frozen strawberries, but fresh would also work well.

5 ounces vanilla yogurt
½ cup brewed coffee, cooled
½ cup milk
1 cup ice
½ teaspoon vanilla
1½ tablespoons unsweetened cocoa powder
1 cup strawberries (fresh or frozen)
1 tablespoon chocolate chips

Add all ingredients to a blender and process until the ice and berries are broken up and the mixture is smooth. Serve immediately.

Peanut Butter Mocha Smoothie

Makes 2 servings

Do you ever find yourself really wanting a milk shake but you don't have any ice cream? This is one of my solutions when I find myself in a jam. It's still pretty healthy—not too heavy—but it tastes like dessert. Of course, if you did have ice cream, this would also be delicious with a scoop of vanilla or chocolate added in . . . but you didn't hear that from me.

½ cup yogurt
½ cup brewed coffee, cooled
½ cup milk
2 tablespoons smooth peanut butter
1 tablespoon unsweetened cocoa powder
½ teaspoon vanilla
1 cup ice
chocolate syrup, for glass or topping

Add all ingredients to a blender and process until the ice is broken up and the mixture is smooth. Serve immediately in a chocolate syrup–swirled glass (optional).

Mint Mocha

Makes 1 serving

If I could eat one combination for the rest of my life, it would be mint and chocolate. I have always loved anything mint chocolate and still do! It was only a matter of time before I added some mint to a mocha, and it was a great decision. This recipe is to make a hot mocha, but you could also mix up the mocha base and stir it into your cold brew for an iced mint mocha, or use it in hot chocolate, too.

1 tablespoon unsweetened cocoa powder
1 tablespoon sugar
¼ teaspoon peppermint extract
1 tablespoon water
1 cup hot coffee, freshly brewed
½ cup milk, heated or steamed
chocolate syrup, for drizzling

In the bottom of a large glass or coffee mug, stir the cocoa powder, sugar, peppermint extract, and water together until the cocoa is dissolved.

Pour in the coffee, followed by the hot milk (and foam, if you have a steamer).

Top with chocolate syrup before serving.

Homemade Irish Cream

Makes about 3 cups

Out of all the recipes in this cookbook, I'm fairly sure that this is in the top three. When I was working on this recipe, I didn't know how much I would end up enjoying it, but it has become a staple in our house and I will never buy Irish cream again! That's how good this is. I use heavy cream from a local dairy that is super thick and creamy, and I make sure to use a good quality whiskey that we drink on its own. The better quality you start out with, the better the end result!

1 cup heavy cream
1 tablespoon instant espresso
1 tablespoon unsweetened cocoa powder
⅔ cup whiskey
2 teaspoons vanilla extract
1 (14-ounce) can sweetened condensed milk

In a medium bowl, mix 2 tablespoons of the cream with the instant espresso and cocoa powder until the mixture is smooth. Add in the rest of the cream.

Gently stir in the whiskey, vanilla extract, and sweetened condensed milk.

Pour into a large jar or other airtight container and chill until ready to serve.

Homemade Kahlua

Makes 1 bottle

I love finding ways to make typically store-bought items even better at home! This homemade Kahlua is ten times better than anything you can get at the store, especially when you start with your favorite coffee beans and good liquor. This, along with the Irish cream, make for great host/hostess or holiday gifts.

1 750-milliliter bottle vodka
1⅓ cups dark rum
1⅓ cups sugar
⅔ pound whole coffee beans
1 vanilla bean

Pour all the ingredients together in a large, airtight container or jar. Shake vigorously to mix everything together and help the sugar to dissolve.

Place a label on the container and let it sit in a dark, cool place for 3–4 weeks. Shake or stir the mixture a few times a week.

Strain the liqueur through a cheesecloth or coffee filters over a colander to remove the vanilla bean and coffee beans. Store in a clean airtight container. This will last months, or even years, as long as it is sealed when not being used.

SAUCES, DIPS, AND TOPPINGS

Now that you know how to make a great cup of coffee, here's some new ways to use it in both sweet and savory sauces, dips, and toppings. Ever think about adding coffee to your barbeque sauce? Now you will. Coffee isn't just for sweet dishes!

Coffee Maple Barbeque Sauce

Makes about 2 cups

Homemade barbeque sauce is a great way to get started on using coffee in savory recipes. One, it's extremely easy to make, and two, the coffee is the perfect balance with the tart tomatoes and vinegar, sweet maple syrup, and bevy of spices going on!

½ cup ketchup
1 cup tomato sauce
⅔ cup brewed coffee, chilled
⅓ cup apple cider vinegar
¼ cup maple syrup
¼ cup Worcestershire sauce
2 tablespoons tomato paste
2 tablespoons Dijon mustard
1 tablespoon onion powder
1 tablespoon garlic powder
1 tablespoon instant espresso
1½ teaspoons cayenne pepper
1 teaspoon salt
½ teaspoon pepper

Mix all the ingredients together in a saucepan. Bring to a simmer and cook, covered, about 15 minutes. Use immediately or cool and refrigerate until ready to use.

Java Vanilla Fruit Dip

Makes 1 cup dip

I love having fruit as an afternoon snack, but sometimes, you just need a little something extra along with it. This fruit dip is much healthier than some of the other marshmallow-fluff based options and just as tasty! I love using whole milk plain yogurt because it's not as tart as the fat-free versions, but feel free to use whatever yogurt you like!

½ cup plain yogurt
½ cup plain whole milk yogurt
1 tablespoon instant espresso
1 tablespoon pure maple syrup
1 teaspoon vanilla extract

Mix all the ingredients in a bowl. Serve immediately with fruit and cookies.

Sweet and Salty Ice Cream Topping

Makes about 1 cup total

Again with the sweet and salty? Yes! This mix might not be something you've seen at your local ice cream shop, but it should be! It has all my favorite things: chocolate sprinkles, great coffee, brown sugar, chocolate chips, and sea salt—the perfect topping for your favorite scoop of ice cream.

1 ounce chocolate sprinkles
2 tablespoons ground coffee of your choice
4 tablespoons brown sugar
2 tablespoons mini chocolate chips
1½ teaspoons sea salt

Mix all the ingredients together, breaking up any clumps of brown sugar. Sprinkle on ice cream or yogurt for a salty-sweet bite!

Coffee Caramel Sauce

Makes about 1 ½ cups sauce

Any time you have a homemade caramel sauce, you know it's going to be a good thing. Adding coffee to an already delicious caramel sauce? That takes it over the top! I especially love this drizzled over scoops of chocolate and coffee ice cream.

1⅓ cups sugar
⅓ cup water
1 cup heavy cream
2 tablespoons brewed coffee, cooled
2 teaspoons instant espresso
1 tablespoon salted butter
1 teaspoon salt

Mix the sugar and water in a heavy saucepan over medium heat, whisking until the sugar is completely dissolved. Bring the mixture to a boil, letting it cook until it turns a golden brown, about 10–20 minutes.

Once the syrup has a nice golden brown color, remove the pan from the heat and stir in the heavy cream. The mixture will bubble up and splatter. Let the mixture settle before stirring.

Return the pan to low heat, and stir in the brewed coffee, instant espresso, butter, and salt. Serve immediately and warm, or cool in the refrigerator until ready to use.

Chocolate-Coffee Gravy

Makes about 1 cup

This recipe has a special place in my heart. My Nanny used to make her "chocolate sauce," which was this gravy (minus the coffee), and spread it on saltines as a treat for my dad and his brothers when they were growing up. It's so simple, and so easy, but also really tasty and a fun little treat to have in your recipe arsenal. And since Nanny was a big coffee fan, I think she would have loved this version.

1 cup powdered sugar
2 tablespoons unsweetened cocoa powder
½ teaspoon vanilla extract
pinch salt
2–3 tablespoons brewed coffee, cooled

In a small bowl, mix the powdered sugar with the cocoa powder, vanilla, and salt. Add in the coffee and stir until the mixture is smooth, adding more coffee if the sauce is too thick.

Serve spread on saltine crackers, just like my Nanny did.

Espresso Butter

Makes about ¼ cup

Compound butter isn't a new idea, but if you haven't made your own flavored butter at home yet, you should! All you need is some softened butter and something to mix in. You can make savory herb butters to use on biscuits or steak or stirred into rice or pasta. Or you can make sweet butters for pancakes, waffles, or muffins, like this espresso butter. This isn't necessarily sweet—there's no sugar added—but the addition of espresso in the salted butter gives it a deep, complex flavor that is perfect on my espresso banana muffins, or just spread on toast!

1 stick salted butter, softened to room temperature
1½ teaspoons instant espresso

Mash the softened butter with the instant espresso until the espresso flakes are equally mixed in. Either scoop into serving dish or roll into a log shape and wrap with plastic wrap. Chill until ready to use.

This butter goes well with the Espresso Banana Muffins on page 29.

Spiced Whipped Cream

Makes about 2 cups

Everyone loves whipped cream, right? Well, everyone should love homemade whipped cream. Especially when you add just the right amount of sugar, a pinch of espresso, and some nutmeg for good measure. Try this on the coffee granita or on ice cream or even with your waffles for an indulgent weekend breakfast!

1 cup heavy cream
2 teaspoons sugar
½ teaspoon instant espresso
⅛ teaspoon ground nutmeg

Beat the heavy cream until it starts to form soft peaks, about 4–6 minutes. Add in the sugar, espresso, and nutmeg, and beat for another 1–2 minutes until the cream is thick and forms stiff peaks.

This cream goes well with Coffee Granita on page 139.

Makes about 1 ½ cups sauce

I think, out of all the recipes I tested for this cookbook, this is my husband's favorite. In fact, we ended up making this sauce recipe three or four times in one week, just because we loved it so much! Classic mole sauces can take a long time to cook (and they're totally worth it!), but this is a great, quick alternative when you want this flavor, but need it fast.

¾ cup crushed tomatoes
2 chipotle peppers in adobo sauce
½ medium onion, chopped into large chunks
2 garlic cloves
¼ cup pepitas or almonds
2 tablespoons unsweetened cocoa powder
1 teaspoon instant espresso
1 teaspoon salt
½ teaspoon cumin
½ teaspoon oregano
½ teaspoon coriander
½ teaspoon cinnamon
½ teaspoon black pepper
½ cup water
½ cup brewed coffee, cooled

Add all the ingredients to a blender or food processor and turn on low, puréeing the sauce until it's mostly smooth. Store in the refrigerator until ready to use.

Spiced Coffee Marinade

Makes about ½ cup, enough to marinate 1 pound of meat

My husband is the grill master in our household. I love having him grill meals because it's less cleanup and less work in the kitchen, and he loves it because he gets to cook over fire. It's a win-win! This is a twist on a marinade that he uses fairly often on steaks and pork chops. The coffee, balsamic vinegar, and ancho chili powder add great flavor to any grilled meat and balance one another out nicely.

¼ cup brewed coffee, cooled
1 tablespoon Worcestershire sauce
1 tablespoon olive oil
1 tablespoon balsamic vinegar
1 teaspoon ancho chili powder
½ teaspoon garlic powder
½ teaspoon onion powder
½ teaspoon salt
¼ teaspoon black pepper

Mix all the ingredients together and pour over beef or pork. Let the meat marinate at least 30 minutes or up to 8 hours/overnight before grilling.

This rub is used in the Smoky Coffee Marinated Pork Chops on page 103.

Mocha Icing

Makes about 1 cup

Any time our family had a birthday growing up, my Mammaw or Mom would make homemade chocolate cake with homemade chocolate icing. But their icing wasn't the super thick and sugary buttercream-type icing. It was a thin layer of perfectly sweet cocoa icing, just how I like it. This mocha version is fun for a little twist on your typical chocolate icing for cake or cupcakes.

2 tablespoons butter, melted
2 tablespoons unsweetened cocoa powder
2 tablespoons brewed coffee
½ teaspoon vanilla
1¼ cups powdered sugar

In a small bowl, mix the melted butter with the cocoa powder, coffee, and vanilla.

Stir in the powdered sugar until everything is combined. If you'd like the frosting a little thicker, add some more powdered sugar, one spoonful at a time.

Note: This is more of a pourable/spoonable frosting rather than a thick, fluffy buttercream. It will coat the tops of the cupcakes well, but won't make for inches-tall frosting layers.

Use this icing with the cupcakes on page 133!

Quick Ranchero Sauce

Makes about 2 cups sauce

I am all about the quick sauces. I love having a pot of sauce simmering on the stove on a lazy weekend afternoon, but there's not always time for that. This quick ranchero sauce comes together in minutes and is perfect for your favorite Mexican make-at-home meals from tacos to fajitas to enchiladas.

1½ cups crushed tomatoes
½ cup vegetable broth
½ cup brewed coffee, cooled
1 tablespoon brown sugar
2 teaspoons chili powder
1½ teaspoons garlic powder
1½ teaspoons onion powder
1½ teaspoons oregano
½ teaspoon salt
½ teaspoon black pepper

Mix all the ingredients together and let the mixture sit at least 10 minutes before using. This one can be stored in the refrigerator up to a week.

Turn to page 89 to use this Ranchero Sauce in Chicken Enchiladas!

Vanilla Maple Glaze

Makes about 1 cup

This glaze was made to drizzle over waffles, but honestly, it's good on anything. Try it on pancakes, cinnamon rolls, scones, or biscuits.

1½ cups powdered sugar
1 tablespoon pure maple syrup
2 tablespoons brewed, chilled coffee
½ teaspoon vanilla bean paste
1–2 tablespoons milk, to thin glaze

In a medium bowl, mix the powdered sugar with the maple syrup, coffee, and vanilla bean paste. Add 1–2 tablespoons (or more) of milk until the glaze is as thick as you'd like.

Coffee Maple Vinaigrette

Makes about ¹/₂ cup dressing

A few years ago, I fell in love with a maple vinaigrette dressing and since then, I haven't been able to stop thinking of ways to make it even more delicious. Whenever I think of maple syrup, I automatically think of coffee, as well. Maybe because maple syrup is usually a part of breakfast and coffee is definitely a part of breakfast. The coffee provides the perfect base for this dressing, but it's not overwhelming. Even non–coffee drinkers will love this salad dressing!

2 tablespoons brewed coffee, cooled
1 tablespoon balsamic vinegar
1 tablespoon pure maple syrup
4 tablespoons olive oil
1 teaspoon Dijon mustard
¼ teaspoon salt
⅛ teaspoon black pepper

Whisk all ingredients together until the Dijon is incorporated. Serve over your favorite salad. This dressing goes especially well with goat or feta cheese, apples, dried cherries or other dried fruits, and nuts. The dressing itself is fairly balanced, so it really can go with any salad where you'd normally use a vinaigrette.

SAVORIES

The savory recipes. Finally! I'm sure it will be surprising that you can use coffee in these dishes, but I promise—the coffee adds such great flavor and depth to the dishes. Even if you think it sounds strange to add coffee in your enchilada or barbeque recipe, try it. You won't be sorry.

Chicken Enchiladas with Quick Coffee Ranchero Sauce

Makes 4-6 servings

If you're looking for a great savory recipe to start out with, these enchiladas are quick and easy! I usually get a rotisserie chicken to save myself even more time on busy weeknights, but you could also cook a batch of chicken on the weekends and have it ready to go. The sauce is sweet and smoky, and the enchiladas come together in no time.

Sauce
1½ cups crushed tomatoes
½ cup broth
½ cup brewed coffee, chilled
1 tablespoon brown sugar
1½ teaspoons garlic powder
1½ teaspoons onion powder
2 teaspoons chili powder
½ teaspoon salt
½ teaspoon pepper

Enchiladas
8–9 corn or flour tortillas
2 cups cooked chicken, chopped
1 cup cheese, shredded
¼ cup scallions
¼ cup cilantro

Preheat oven to 350°F.

Mix all the sauce ingredients together.

Spoon about 3 tablespoons of the sauce into the bottom of a 9 x 13 baking dish.

Heat the tortillas in the microwave, covered with a damp paper towel, for 20–30 seconds.

Take 1 tortilla, add about 3–4 spoonfuls of chicken and a spoonful of sauce. Roll up the tortilla and place seam-side down in the pan. Repeat until all the tortillas and chicken are used and pan is full.

Top the enchiladas with more sauce and the cheese.

Bake 25–30 minutes. Sprinkle the scallions and cilantro over the top and serve.

Crockpot Pulled Barbeque Chicken

Makes 6-8 servings

I love my crock pot. Do you love your crockpot? It's so nice to be able to throw ingredients in the bowl in the morning and let it do all the work for me. We serve this pulled barbeque chicken on buns, with or without slaw, and use it on pizzas (my favorite way to have it!). The sauce cooks and thickens while it soaks into the chicken all day, giving everything a sweet and spicy barbeque flavor.

½ cup ketchup
1 cup tomato sauce
⅔ cup brewed coffee, chilled
⅓ cup apple cider vinegar
¼ cup maple syrup
¼ cup Worcestershire sauce
2 tablespoons tomato paste
2 tablespoons Dijon mustard

1 tablespoon onion powder
1 tablespoon garlic powder
1 tablespoon instant espresso
1½ teaspoons cayenne pepper
1 teaspoon salt
½ teaspoon pepper
1½ pounds boneless, skinless chicken breast

Mix all the sauce ingredients (except the chicken) together in the bottom of the crockpot. Nestle the chicken into the sauce, spooning some of the sauce over the top of the meat.

Cook on high for 2 hours or low for 4 hours.

Remove the chicken from the pot and shred the meat using two forks.

Return the meat to the sauce and cook another 30–40 minutes.

Coffee Braised Ribs

Makes 4 servings

To be honest, I've always been a little scared to cook ribs at home by myself. We've cooked ribs before, but I usually leave things like this to my husband to do on the grill. But I have to say: cooking ribs in the crockpot and then finishing them in the oven may be my favorite way to have them now. The ribs cook slowly, which leaves them super tender and juicy, and then you just slather on some sauce and crisp them up a little in the oven before serving. So easy!

3 pounds ribs, trimmed to fit in crockpot
1 teaspoon salt
1 teaspoon pepper
½ cup water
½ cup brewed coffee
1 onion, quartered
1 cup barbeque sauce (your favorite, or the recipe on page 69)

Season the ribs with the salt and pepper.

Pour the water and coffee into the bottom of the crockpot.

Place the ribs in the liquid. Top with the onion.

Cook on high 4 hours or on low 7–8 hours.

When you're ready to eat, preheat oven to 375°F.

Place the ribs on a baking sheet and brush both sides with barbeque sauce.

Bake 10–15 minutes.

Coffee Braised Pot Roast

Makes 8–10 servings

Another slow-cooked recipe! For things like roasts and ribs, I love using either my crockpot or a big Dutch oven when I'm home on the weekends and have time to let it cook slowly. You really can't rush cooking a large piece of meat—it needs time and liquid to cook through and become tender. I love serving this pot roast with mashed or roasted potatoes.

1 (3 to 4-pound) beef roast (round, chuck)
1 tablespoon olive oil
1½ teaspoons salt
¾ teaspoon pepper
2 tablespoons tomato paste
1 cup brewed coffee, cooled
2½ cups beef broth
1 bay leaf

Place a large stockpot or Dutch oven over medium heat and get your crockpot ready.

Season the roast on all sides with salt and pepper.

Heat the oil in the pot or Dutch oven, then sear the roast on all sides.

Once the roast is browned on each side, move it to your crockpot and add the tomato paste, brewed coffee, beef broth, and bay leaf.

Cook on low in your crockpot for 6–7 hours.

Slice or pull the roast into pieces before serving.

Slow-Cooked Coffee Short Ribs

Makes 4 servings

This is one dish that is best made on a weekend if you work away from the house during the week. The short ribs are started on the stove top, to brown the meat and vegetables, and then cooked slow and low in the oven until the meat is falling off the bone. The best part about cooking something slow and low all afternoon? Your house will smell incredible all day!

2 teaspoons olive oil
2 pounds beef or buffalo short ribs
1 tablespoon salt
2 teaspoons black pepper
1 medium onion, diced
2 carrots, diced

2 garlic cloves, chopped
2 cups red wine
1 cup beef broth
1 cup brewed coffee
2 bay leaves
1–2 sprigs fresh rosemary

Preheat the oven to 375°F.

Heat a large, heavy pot over medium-high heat and add the olive oil.

Season the short ribs with salt and pepper and add them to the pan, flipping the ribs every 3–4 minutes until all sides are browned.

Remove the ribs from the pan and set aside. Add the onion, carrots, and garlic to the pot and cook, scraping the bits from the bottom of the pot.

Once the vegetables have started to soften (about 3–5 minutes), pour in the red wine, beef broth, and coffee. Add the bay leaves and rosemary and place the ribs back in the pot with the rest of the ingredients.

Bring the mixture to a simmer on the stove top, put the lid on the pot, and then place it in the oven.

Cook at 375°F for 2½ hours. Remove the lid and cook for another 30–45 minutes until the sauce has reduced a little more and the short ribs are tender.

Mocha Mole Chili

Makes 6-8 servings

Chili peppers are one ingredient that go really well with coffee. I think it's the combination of the spice and heat with the fruity, tart, or smoky aspects of the coffee that balance each other out. So using coffee in a big pot of chili is a no-brainer! I also like to toss in a spoonful of cocoa powder and some hominy for some extra sweetness.

½ pound ground beef
1 (15-ounce) can dark red kidney beans, drained and rinsed
2 (15-ounce) cans light red kidney beans, drained and rinsed
1 (15-ounce) can hominy, drained
1 (15-ounce) can crushed tomatoes
1 cup brewed coffee
½ cup water
1 tablespoon unsweetened cocoa powder
1 tablespoon ancho chili powder
2 teaspoons garlic powder
2 teaspoons onion powder
1 teaspoon salt
1 teaspoon smoked paprika
½ teaspoon pepper
½ teaspoon cayenne

Place a large pot over medium heat.

Crumble the ground beef into the pan and cook, stirring occasionally, 5–7 minutes until the meat is browned and cooked through.

Pour in all the remaining ingredients and bring the chili to a simmer.

Cook, over low heat, 30 minutes to 1 hour.

Spiced Grilled Steak Tacos

Makes 4 servings

Using coffee in meat marinades was actually one of the first ways I ever used it in savory dishes. This marinade takes all my favorite Mexican flavors—chilis, garlic, oregano, lime juice—and combines them with espresso and some brewed coffee to make the most flavorful, juicy steak for steak tacos.

1½–2 pounds flank steak
1 tablespoon instant espresso
2 teaspoons ancho chili powder
1 teaspoon garlic powder
1 teaspoon onion powder
1 teaspoon salt
1 teaspoon oregano
½ teaspoon black pepper
2 tablespoons brewed coffee, cooled
1 tablespoon olive oil

1 tablespoon lime juice
½ tablespoon Worcestershire sauce
¼ cup cilantro, chopped
½ cup scallions, sliced
½ cup radishes, sliced
1 cup lettuce
½ avocado, diced
¼–½ cup salsa
corn or flour tortillas (for serving)

Place the steak in a large bowl or resealable bag.

In a small bowl, mix the espresso, chili powder, garlic powder, onion powder, salt, oregano, black pepper, coffee, olive oil, lime juice, and Worcestershire sauce.

Add the spice mixture to the steak and toss until the steak is coated. Let the steak sit in the marinade for at least 30 minutes.

Set your grill to a medium-high heat.

Grill the steak 4–6 minutes on each side until medium well, or to your desired doneness.

Remove the steak from the grill, cover the steak, and let it rest 5–10 minutes before slicing.

Top your choice of tortillas with thin slices of the grilled steak, cilantro, scallions, radishes, lettuce, avocado, and salsa.

Coffee and Chili Roasted Veggies

Makes 4–6 servings

One surefire way to make sure we eat all the vegetables in the fridge is to make a big pan of roasted veggies at some point during the week. The instant espresso adds just a hint of bitter smokiness, which is balanced by the paprika and garlic. Plus, the carrots and onions get sweeter as they cook, adding an even greater depth of flavor.

5 carrots, peeled and cut into 1-inch pieces
½ large head cauliflower, cut into bite-sized pieces
1 red onion, cut into 1-inch pieces
2 teaspoons instant espresso
½ teaspoon ancho chili powder
½ teaspoon sweet paprika
½ teaspoon garlic powder
½ teaspoon salt
¼ teaspoon black pepper
¼ teaspoon dried thyme
2 tablespoons olive oil

Preheat oven to 400°F.

Toss the chopped veggies with all the spices and the olive oil.

Place in a single layer on a baking sheet and roast for 25–35 minutes.

Sweet and Spicy Beef

Makes 4-6 servings

I made a slightly different version of this recipe on my blog a few years ago, and it has turned into one of the most popular recipes that I've ever posted. This is a quick, easy to make meal that we cook quite a bit. The most important thing is to make sure you add the crushed red pepper and brown sugar—you want that balance of heat and sweet in the finished dish.

1 tablespoon olive oil
1½ pounds ground beef
1 clove garlic, minced
1 teaspoon salt
1 teaspoon crushed red pepper
½ teaspoon black pepper
⅓ cup Worcestershire sauce
⅓ cup brown sugar
¼ cup brewed coffee
½ cup scallions, sliced
rice (for serving)

Heat a skillet over medium heat and add the olive oil.

Brown the ground beef and cook, breaking up, 5–7 minutes, until it is cooked through.

Add in the garlic, salt, crushed red pepper, black pepper, Worcestershire sauce, brown sugar, coffee, and scallions.

Let the mixture cook until most of the liquid has been cooked into the meat.

Serve over rice with more scallions.

Makes 4 servings

I couldn't have a coffee cookbook without doing some type of redeye gravy. And, having grown up in the South, I know you can't have redeye gravy without ham and grits. Although this recipe sounds like it might take a while to make, it actually comes together really quickly! The ham just needs to brown, and I use quick-cooking grits (not instant) that only take a few minutes.

1 pound lean ham steaks
1 tablespoon butter
½ medium onion, finely diced
2 tablespoons flour
1 cup brewed coffee
½ cup broth, any variety (chicken, beef, vegetable)
2 tablespoons heavy cream
½ teaspoon salt
¼ teaspoon black pepper

For the grits
1½ cups milk
1½ cups water
¾ cup quick-cooking grits
½ cup cheddar, shredded
½ teaspoon salt
½ teaspoon black pepper

Place a skillet over medium heat. Brown the ham steaks in the pan on both sides. Once the ham is cooked through, remove them from the pan.

Add the butter and onion to the pan and cook, stirring occasionally, until the onion is softened, about 2–3 minutes. Stir in the flour and let the flour cook into the onions.

Slowly pour in the coffee and broth. Bring the mixture to a simmer, and let the gravy thicken, about 5 minutes. Remove the pan from heat and stir in the cream, salt, and pepper.

While the ham and gravy are cooking, bring the milk and water to a boil in a medium pot. Slowly stir in the grits, lower the heat to low, and cover the pot. Cook the grits for 5 minutes, until thickened, stirring occasionally.

Remove the pan from heat; stir in the cheese, salt, and pepper. Serve topped with a ham steak and gravy.

Smoky Coffee Marinated Pork Chops

Makes 2 servings

One of our favorite local restaurants has completely spoiled me for pork chops. They always have incredible, thick bone-in pork chops, usually stuffed with something, and that's the only way I like them now. Good-bye, sad little thin chops—hello, super thick, tender, perfectly cooked pork. I don't try to top their stuffed recipes, but this coffee based marinade is a great option for a quick grilled meal at home.

¼ cup brewed coffee, cooled
1 tablespoon Worcestershire sauce
1 tablespoon olive oil
1 tablespoon balsamic vinegar
1 teaspoon ancho chili powder
½ teaspoon garlic powder
½ teaspoon onion powder
½ teaspoon salt
¼ teaspoon black pepper
2 large bone-in pork chops

Mix all the ingredients together and pour over pork chops. Let the meat marinate at least 30 minutes or up to 8 hours/overnight before grilling.

Grill over medium-high heat until the pork is cooked through.

Roasted Mole Chicken

Makes 4 servings

This was my husband's favorite recipe out of everything I made for this cookbook. We ate this exact meal four times in one week, and I made more mole sauce than I ever thought I would in that amount of time. The sauce is whipped up in a blender or food processor, and the chicken is the only thing you need to cook, so it's a great option any day of the week.

1¼ pounds boneless, skinless chicken breast
1 batch quick mole sauce (recipe on page 80)
corn tortillas and avocados, for serving

Preheat your oven to 425°F.

Slice the chicken into 4–8 pieces that are equal thickness so they will cook for the same amount of time.

Toss the chicken with 1 cup of the mole sauce. Let the chicken marinate at least 30 minutes.

Place the chicken on a parchment-lined baking sheet, brush with a little extra sauce, and cook 25–30 minutes.

Serve topped with extra sauce, tortillas, and avocado.

Makes 10–12 servings

The inspiration for this soup recipe is one that was handed to me from one of my husband's cousins, and it has quickly become a family favorite. It really is the perfect black bean soup—not completely creamy, but not too chunky. Everything is cooked just right, and the bacon and coffee add just the right amount of smokiness. I always top my bowl with fresh lime juice, diced avocado, and some shredded cheese . . . plus a few tortilla chips thrown in for good measure.

4 slices bacon
2 tablespoons olive oil
2 medium onions, chopped
3 carrots, diced
3 celery ribs, sliced
4 cloves garlic, minced
1 teaspoon crushed red pepper flakes
1 tablespoon tomato paste
2 tablespoons balsamic vinegar
2 tablespoons Worcestershire sauce

1 (28-ounce) can crushed tomatoes
2 tablespoons cumin
2 tablespoons smoked paprika
3½ cups chicken or vegetable broth
1½ cups brewed coffee
4 (15-ounce) cans black beans, rinsed and
    drained
2 tablespoons cornstarch
2 tablespoons water
2 tablespoons fresh lime juice

Dice bacon and add to a large pot over medium heat.

Once the bacon starts releasing its fat, add in the olive oil, onions, carrots, and celery and cook together 3–5 minutes until the vegetables begin to soften.

Stir in the garlic, crushed red pepper flakes, and tomato paste and cook for another 2–3 minutes.

Pour in the balsamic vinegar, Worcestershire sauce, crushed tomatoes, cumin, smoked paprika, broth, coffee, and beans.

Bring the soup to a boil, cover the pot, and lower the heat to a simmer. Cook 20–30 minutes.

Mix the cornstarch with 2 tablespoons of water and pour the mixture into the soup. Let it cook another 5–10 minutes until slightly thickened.

Stir in the lime juice before serving. You can also purée part of the soup if you'd like it a little creamier.

Spicy Roasted Potatoes

Makes 4 servings

My mom makes great roasted potatoes. I still think that my best batches never turn out as good as hers, but these are probably the closest I've come. The key is to not use too much oil (so they don't get soggy) and a good coating of spices that get toasted along with the potatoes.

1½ pounds Yukon gold potatoes
1 tablespoon olive oil
1 tablespoon instant espresso
2 teaspoons ancho chili powder
2 teaspoons garlic powder
2 teaspoons onion powder
1 teaspoon sweet paprika
1 teaspoon salt
½ teaspoon black pepper
¼ teaspoon cayenne pepper

Preheat the oven to 425°F.

Dice the potatoes into ½-inch pieces.

Toss the potatoes with the olive oil and spices.

Place in a single layer on a parchment-lined baking sheet and bake at 425°F for 25–35 minutes or until cooked through.

Pulled Beef Sandwiches

Makes 4-6 servings

Somehow, I always end up with a few packages of stew beef in the freezer and not enough ways to use it up. There's only so many times you want a big pot of beef stew. Pulled beef sandwiches to the rescue! I normally would only think to use a big roast for a dish like this, but the stew beef worked so well that it'll be my go-to for pulled beef from now on. Again, the crockpot does the work for you in this one—all you have to do is shred the meat and put together your sandwiches.

2 pounds stew beef
1 cup brewed coffee
1 cup red wine
1 garlic clove, crushed
1 teaspoon salt

½ teaspoon black pepper
8–10 slices bread
¼ cup mayonnaise
1–1½ cups mozzarella cheese
fresh parsley

Place the beef, coffee, wine, garlic, salt, and pepper in a crockpot. Cook the beef on low 6–7 hours or until it easily falls apart.

Remove the crushed garlic clove and throw away.

Shred the beef using two forks.

Preheat the oven to 350°F.

Take each slice of bread and top with a small smear of mayonnaise.

Top each slice with some of the shredded beef and some of the shredded cheese.

Bake the sandwiches for 10–15 minutes until the cheese is melted and beginning to brown.

Sprinkle with fresh parsley.

Makes 6-8 servings

I've tried a lot of beef stews and nothing can touch this one. Some are just too thin, some are way too thick, and some just aren't that great. This one is still fairly simple—mostly just beef, vegetables, and a roux to thicken it up—but the roux is the secret to a great beef stew! Cooking your roux separately and then adding it to the pot with everything else makes such a difference and doesn't take too much extra time. And definitely don't leave out the Parmesan. I know it might sound strange, but that little bit of salty cheesiness is exactly what beef stew needs to take it over the top.

2 teaspoons olive oil
2 pounds stew beef
2 large Yukon gold potatoes, peeled and diced in 1-inch pieces
1 medium onion, diced
2 cups carrots, diced
3 stalks celery, sliced
2 quarts water
½ cup butter
½ cup all-purpose flour

¾ cup milk
½ cup brewed coffee
¼ cup Parmesan cheese, grated
¼ cup Worcestershire sauce
¼ cup dark beer
2 teaspoons salt
2 teaspoons instant espresso
1 teaspoon black pepper
1 teaspoon dried rosemary

In a large pot, heat the olive oil over medium heat. Add the stew beef and cook, flipping every 2–3 minutes, until the beef is browned on all sides. Remove the beef from the pot.

Add the potatoes, onion, carrots, celery, and water, and bring to a boil. Cook about 10–15 minutes until the vegetables are just tender.

In a separate saucepan, melt the butter. Stir in the flour and cook, whisking constantly, until the mixture has cooked together and is bubbling. Let the roux cook for 3–4 minutes, stirring constantly.

Slowly add the milk, brewed coffee, and Parmesan cheese to the thickened roux, stirring to make sure everything is incorporated. When everything is mixed together and the mixture is nice and thick, remove the pan from heat.

Gently stir the roux into the pot with the vegetables and bring to a low boil. Add in the Worcestershire sauce, beer, salt, instant espresso, black pepper, and rosemary. Let the stew simmer another 5–10 minutes until the stew has thickened and the veggies are completely tender.

SWEETS & SNACKS

Sweets and snacks—the section you've been waiting for! This is probably where most people would think to use coffee as an ingredient, and it's for a good reason! Coffee and chocolate, especially, are two ingredients that are meant to be together. Coffee brings out the subtleties in chocolate, making it even more flavorful, and vice versa. You really can't go wrong if you add coffee to a sweet dish, no matter what it is.

Orange Mocha Pudding Cups

Makes 4 servings

I'm all about easy desserts. Cookies are a mainstay in our house, which are pretty simple, but having other options like these pudding cups are fun to switch it up. Plus, they're made entirely in a blender and then set in the fridge, so there's almost no hands-on time!

⅔ cup whole milk
1 egg
2 tablespoons sugar
2 tablespoons brewed, chilled coffee
1 teaspoon orange zest
¼ teaspoon salt
1 cup semisweet chocolate chips

Heat the milk on the stovetop until the edges are bubbling.

While the milk is heating, put the remaining ingredients in a blender and process on low until the egg is beaten and the chocolate chips are chopped up.

Once the milk is heated, remove it from the stovetop and, while the blender is running on low, slowly stream in the hot milk. Let the blender run until you've poured in all the milk and mixture is smooth and creamy.

Pour the pudding mixture into 4 coffee mugs or small dishes. Cover with plastic wrap and chill at least 4–5 hours/overnight before serving.

Triple Chip Espresso Cookies

Makes about 3½ dozen cookies

Out of the eleven years that we've been married, I'd say that chocolate chip cookies are the most popular recipe in our house. I've made more cookies over this last decade than any other dish, and I'm not sad about it. Homemade cookies are such a treat. I also love that I can make each batch just a little bit different so we don't get bored. This is a pretty classic cookie dough base, with more brown sugar for a chewier cookie, instant espresso for a punch of coffee, and three different kinds of chocolate chips just because.

2 sticks (1 cup) butter, softened to room temperature
1 cup packed light brown sugar
½ cup granulated sugar
2 eggs
2 teaspoons vanilla extract
½ teaspoon salt
½ teaspoon baking soda
2 tablespoons instant espresso
2¼ cups all-purpose flour
¾ cup semisweet chocolate chips
½ cup white chocolate chips
½ milk or dark chocolate chips

Preheat oven to 350°F.

Cream the butter and the sugars together until light and fluffy. Add in the eggs, one at a time, mixing until completely incorporated.

Add in the vanilla extract, salt, baking soda, espresso, and flour, mixing on low until all the flour is assimilated. Mix in all the chocolate chips.

Drop the mixture by rounded tablespoons onto cookie sheet, and bake 11–13 minutes until golden around the edges and just set in the center.

Coffee Cocoa Crinkle Cookies

Makes about 3 dozen cookies

Light, airy, crispy on the outside, chewy on the inside. These crinkle cookies are a cinch to pull together. Try something different for your next holiday cookie swap or potluck and make these!

3 cups powdered sugar
¾ cup unsweetened cocoa powder
2 tablespoons instant espresso
1 tablespoon cornstarch
¾ teaspoon salt
2 egg whites
1 egg
2 teaspoons vanilla extract
1 cup dark chocolate chips

Preheat oven to 350°F.

In a large bowl, whisk the powdered sugar with the cocoa powder, espresso, cornstarch, and salt. Stir in the egg whites, whole egg, and vanilla. Fold in the chocolate chips.

Drop the dough by tablespoon onto a parchment-lined baking sheet, about 2 inches apart.

Bake 12–14 minutes until puffed and crinkled on top.

Cool 5 minutes before moving to a wire rack.

Irish Cream Truffles

Makes about 20 truffles

Truffles always seem so indulgent to me, which means I think that they're hard to make. But that couldn't be further from the truth. The base doesn't take long to put together, and once it's chilled, all you have to do is roll them out, coat them in a mix of cocoa and coffee, and enjoy!

2 tablespoons heavy cream
6 ounces semisweet chocolate, chopped (or good-quality chips)
2 tablespoons Irish cream
½ teaspoon vanilla extract
⅛ teaspoon salt
½ cup cocoa powder
¼ cup finely ground coffee

Heat the 2 tablespoons cream in a bowl over a pot of simmering water.

Add the chocolate and stir together until chocolate is melted.

Stir in the Irish cream, vanilla, and salt, and remove from heat.

Set the bowl aside and let it cool for 5 minutes. Cover and chill at least 1 hour or until firm but scoopable.

On a plate, mix the cocoa powder with the ground coffee.

Scoop truffles with melon baller or spoon. Roll into rounds and roll through the cocoa/coffee mixture to coat.

No-Churn Coffee Ice Cream

Makes 6 servings

Homemade ice cream doesn't have to be hard or take a lot of time. In fact, you don't even need to have an ice cream maker! As long as you have heavy cream, some sweetened condensed milk, and your favorite flavors to mix in, you're set. This no-churn coffee ice cream has both brewed coffee and instant espresso for double the coffee flavor, and it comes together in no time. Mix it up, toss it in the freezer, and you'll have creamy, rich ice cream in just a few hours.

1½ cups heavy cream
⅔ cup sweetened condensed milk
2 tablespoons brewed, chilled coffee
1 tablespoon instant espresso
1 teaspoon vanilla extract
½ teaspoon salt

In a medium bowl, whisk the heavy cream until it thickens. Gently stir in the remaining ingredients.

Pour the mixture into an airtight container and freeze at least 7 hours.

No-Churn Coffee Cookies 'n 'Cream Ice Cream

Makes 6 servings

If you thought the no-churn coffee ice cream couldn't get any better, you were wrong. I love cookies'n'cream ice cream and knew it would be a great addition to the coffee ice cream base. The sweet vanilla and chocolate flavors in the cookies are the perfect crunchy mix-in with the creamy espresso ice cream.

1½ cups heavy cream
⅔ cup sweetened condensed milk
2 tablespoons brewed, chilled coffee
1 tablespoon instant espresso
1 teaspoon vanilla extract
½ teaspoon salt
1 cup chocolate cream cookies, crushed

In a medium bowl, whisk the heavy cream until it thickens. Gently stir in the remaining ingredients.

Pour the mixture into an airtight container and freeze at least 7 hours.

Roasted Coffee and Spiced Cocoa Nuts

Makes 4 cups, about 12 servings

These nuts are something special. You know those stands that show up in the mall around the holidays, selling all kinds of fancy, candied, and spiced nuts? I talked to a lady that worked at one and got some ideas on how they got that crispy coating on the candied almonds, and this has now turned into a regular holiday treat in our family. We make multiple batches of these every year to give as gifts and they're gobbled up in no time.

2 cups pecan halves
2 cups walnut halves
3 egg whites
1⅓ cups granulated sugar
2 tablespoons instant espresso

1½ tablespoons unsweetened cocoa powder
½ teaspoon cayenne pepper
1 stick butter
1 teaspoon salt

Preheat oven to 325°F.

Place the pecans and walnuts on a baking sheet with a rim and toast in the oven for 5 minutes. Remove them from the oven and let them cool.

In a medium bowl, beat the egg whites. Once soft peaks form, add the sugar in 3 or 4 batches. Mix for another 3–4 minutes until the mixture is glossy and smooth.

Fold in the espresso, cocoa powder, and cayenne pepper. Gently fold in the cooled, toasted nuts.

Cut up the stick of butter and put the pieces on the baking sheet. Place in the oven for about 5 minutes until the butter melts.

Spread out the mixture on the baking sheet. Bake for 8–9 minutes, remove from the oven, and stir the nuts around. Bake for another 8–9 minutes, remove from the oven, and stir again. Sprinkle the salt over the nuts and stir them again.

Bake for 10 more minutes, then cool completely before breaking up into pieces.

No-Bake Mocha Drop Cookies

Makes 30–40 cookies

This recipe is straight out of my childhood. My mom has always made the best no-bake cookies. You may call them preacher cookies or drop cookies, but I will always know them as no-bakes and mine will never *have peanut butter. I know lots of people use peanut butter in theirs, but I just don't think you can beat the classic cocoa version. The instant espresso in these brings out the cocoa flavor, and there's just enough of a hint of coffee for a slight mocha taste.*

1 stick butter
2 cups sugar
½ cup milk
2 cups quick oats
½ cup unsweetened cocoa powder
1½ tablespoons instant espresso
1 teaspoon vanilla extract
¼ teaspoon salt

In a medium sauce pan, melt the butter and add the sugar and milk. Bring the mixture to a rolling boil and let it cook for 3½ minutes. (Use a timer to make sure you let it boil for at least 3 minutes!)

Remove the mixture from the heat and stir in the oats, cocoa, espresso, vanilla, and salt.

Drop the mixture by spoonful onto parchment paper and let them set completely.

Note: This recipe does not work well on muggy, stormy days. Believe me—I've tried.

Classic Chocolate Cupcakes

Makes 1 dozen

I love a light, fluffy cupcake, and these always deliver. These pack a double punch of coffee with both brewed coffee and instant espresso, plus a healthy dose of cocoa powder for a rich, chocolate base. Since I'm not a great cake decorator, I go with a more pourable/spreadable icing rather than a fluffy buttercream—easy and delicious! See page 82 for the Mocha Icing recipe.

¾ cup buttermilk

¼ cup brewed coffee, cooled

¾ cup sugar

2 teaspoons vanilla extract

⅓ cup canola oil

⅓ cup unsweetened cocoa powder

1 cup all-purpose flour

1 tablespoon instant espresso

¾ teaspoon baking soda

½ teaspoon baking powder

¼ teaspoon salt

Preheat oven to 350°F.

Mix the buttermilk, coffee, sugar, vanilla, and oil together in a large mixing bowl.

Add in the dry ingredients and stir until just combined.

Fill cupcake liners ¾ of the way and tap the muffin pan on the counter to remove any air bubbles in the batter.

Bake at 350°F for 15–20 minutes until a toothpick comes out clean.

Let them cool before frosting.

Salted Dark Chocolate Coffee Bark

Makes about 2 cups pieces of bark

Here's another great holiday treat! For the past five years, my husband and I have put together baskets of homemade goodies for our families instead of buying Christmas gifts. We always make homemade toffee, roasted coffee and spiced cocoa nuts, some type of bark, and sugared cranberries. I love making barks because they're so simple: all you have to do is melt chocolate, sprinkle on your toppings, and let it set. That's it! The mix of the dark chocolate with coffee beans and sea salt is one of my all-time favorites.

10 ounces 60% dark chocolate or semisweet
¼ cup whole coffee beans (the fruitier, the better!)
1½ teaspoons large flake sea salt

Over a double boiler or in a microwave-safe bowl, melt the chocolate until it's just warm enough to completely melt when you stir (a few minutes over the double boiler or 1–2 minutes in the microwave, checking every 30 seconds).

Pour the chocolate onto a parchment-lined baking sheet and smooth out into an even layer.

Sprinkle the melted chocolate with the coffee beans and the sea salt.

Let the chocolate set at least 1 hour, then break into bite-sized pieces.

Brown Butter Mocha Crisp Bars

Makes 12-18 servings

Just when you thought a childhood favorite couldn't get any better, brown butter comes into the picture. Have you ever browned butter for a recipe? It makes your house smell like toffee and makes anything you add to it one hundred times more delicious. These crisp bars start out with browned butter that's then mixed with marshmallows, espresso, and vanilla before stirring in the cereal and drizzling with espresso-laced chocolate.

4 tablespoons salted butter
5 cups mini marshmallows
2 teaspoons instant espresso
½ teaspoon vanilla extract
6 cups crisp rice cereal
½ cup semisweet chocolate chips
1 teaspoon instant espresso

Melt the butter in a large pot over medium heat. Let the butter cook 3–5 minutes, stirring occasionally, until the butter begins to brown and smells toasted, like toffee.

Stir in the mini marshmallows, instant espresso, and vanilla until the marshmallows are completely melted.

Remove the pan from heat and stir in the rice cereal.

Press the cereal bar mixture into a greased 9 x 13 pan and press into an even layer.

Melt the chocolate chips and stir in the 1 teaspoon instant espresso. Drizzle the chocolate over the cereal mixture.

Slice into bars once the chocolate has set.

Coffee Granita

Makes 6 servings

Want something cool for dessert? This granita is just what you need on a warm summer evening. You can mix this up in minutes earlier in the day (or a few days before) and let it freeze until you're ready to serve. Just make sure to scrape the mixture frequently to easily scoop out the little crystals.

2 cups brewed coffee, warm
⅓ cup brown sugar
zest from 1 orange
1 teaspoon vanilla extract

In a shallow freezer-safe dish, mix the warm coffee with the brown sugar, orange zest, and vanilla.

Cover the dish and place in the freezer for 1 hour. Remove and scrape mixture with a fork. Place back in the freezer and repeat this scraping step every 30–60 minutes for 3–4 hours, or until the mixture is completely frozen but you can scrape into piles of crystals.

Once frozen, scrape again and scoop into dishes. Serve with spiced whipped cream (page 79).

Cinnamon Coffee Chip Biscotti

Makes 2 dozen cookies

What goes better with coffee than biscotti? They are made for each other: the crunchy biscotti is exactly what you need to dip in a hot cup of coffee. I love the addition of cinnamon in these biscotti. The warmth of the cinnamon goes so well with the espresso and semisweet chocolate.

1 cup sugar
1 teaspoon vanilla extract
3 eggs
2 cups all-purpose flour
¼ cup cornmeal

1½ tablespoons instant espresso
1½ teaspoons baking powder
½ teaspoon cinnamon
½ teaspoon salt
1 cup semisweet chocolate chips

Preheat oven to 325°F.

Beat the sugar with the vanilla and eggs until the mixture is light yellow and all the sugar is mixed in well, about 2–3 minutes.

Mix in the flour, cornmeal, espresso, baking powder, cinnamon, salt, and chocolate chips.

Shape the dough into a loaf, 1–2 inches thick, on a parchment-lined baking sheet, wetting your hands if needed.

Bake for 30 minutes at 325°F. Remove from the oven and let the loaf cool for 5 minutes.

Slice the loaf into ½-inch pieces and lay them cut-side down back on the baking sheet.

Bake the sliced cookies another 20–25 minutes until golden and set.

Coffee Cookies 'n' Cream Mini Cheesecakes

Makes 12 servings

I love cheesecake. It's one of my favorite desserts, but there are very rare times that my husband and I need (or even get close to finishing) an entire cheesecake. That's why these mini cheesecakes are the perfect solution! The filling is quick to mix up, and it's nice to have little bite-sized desserts ready and waiting in the refrigerator.

12 chocolate sandwich cookies
1 (8-ounce) package of Neufchâtel (or cream) cheese, softened to room temperature
4 ounces plain whole milk yogurt
2 tablespoons brewed coffee, cooled
1 teaspoon vanilla extract
⅓ cup sugar
1 egg

Preheat oven to 325°F.

Line a 12-cup muffin tin. Place one cookie in the bottom of each cupcake liner.

In a medium bowl, beat the Neufchâtel (or cream) cheese together with the yogurt.

Add in the coffee, vanilla, sugar, and egg and mix until the mixture is completely smooth.

Fill each liner about ¾ of the way, placing the filling on top of the cookies.

Bake for 25–30 minutes until set.

Cool to room temperature, then chill in the refrigerator until ready to serve.

Raspberry Orange Tiramisu

Makes 8-10 servings

Classic tiramisu sticks with coffee and cocoa flavors, but this mix incorporates both raspberry and orange into the mix. The raspberry liqueur and orange juice add a little bit of sweet and tart to the ladyfingers, balancing out the rich mascarpone. The best thing about tiramisu? It looks fancy, but it's a really easy dessert to put together.

1¼ cups espresso or double strong coffee, brewed and cooled
3 tablespoons raspberry liqueur
3 tablespoons orange juice
6 egg yolks
3 tablespoons sugar

1 pound mascarpone
2 packages ladyfingers (about 20–40, depending on the size)
1 tablespoon unsweetened cocoa powder
½ cup fresh raspberries

Mix the cooled coffee with the raspberry liqueur and orange juice.

In a large mixing bowl, beat the egg yolks with the sugar until the mixture is thickened and pale yellow, about 5–7 minutes.

Mix the mascarpone and 1 tablespoon of the coffee mixture into the yolks.

Take the ladyfingers and dip each one in the coffee mixture for 2–3 seconds, turning over to coat all sides. Using half the cookies to cover the bottom of the pan.

Top the bottom layer of cookies with half the mascarpone mixture.

Repeat with another layer of dipped ladyfinger cookies, then top with the rest of the mascarpone.

Cover the pan and let it set in the refrigerator at least 2 hours or overnight.

Dust the top of the tiramisu with the cocoa powder and top with fresh raspberries before serving.

Easy Mocha Mousse

Makes 3-4 cups mousse, 6-8 servings

This may be a cheater's mousse, but I still love it. If you ever find yourself in need a dessert—and fast—this is a great recipe to have on hand. If you have some chocolate and coffee beans in the pantry and heavy cream in the fridge, you'll never be caught without a sweet ending to a meal!

2 cups heavy cream, divided
3 tablespoons coffee beans, cracked/crushed
4 ounces dark or semisweet chocolate
1 teaspoon vanilla extract
pinch salt (less than ⅛ teaspoon)

Heat ½ cup of the cream with the cracked coffee beans in a small saucepan until bubbles start to form around the edges. Remove the pan from heat and strain the beans out of the cream.

Pour the warm cream over the chocolate and let it sit 2–3 minutes, then stir until the chocolate is completely melted into the cream. Let this mixture cool until almost room temperature.

Beat the remaining 1½ cups cream until soft peaks form. Pour in the cooled chocolate mixture, vanilla, and salt. Beat again for another 2–3 minutes until the cream is thickened and the chocolate is fully incorporated.

Chill before serving.

No-Bake Irish Cream Mousse Pie

Makes 8 servings

Everyone needs an easy pie recipe in their arsenal. There are always times when you just need something that's fast and easy to put together, last-minute, or just for those times when you want something fabulous but don't want to spend a ton of time in the kitchen. This pie is exactly what you're looking for! The crust is no-bake, and the mousse comes together in almost no time.

24 chocolate sandwich cookies
4 tablespoons butter, melted
2 cups heavy cream, divided
3 tablespoons coffee beans, cracked/crushed

4 ounces dark or semisweet chocolate
2 tablespoons whiskey
1 teaspoon vanilla extract
pinch salt (less than ⅛ teaspoon)

Crush the cookies in a food processor until finely chopped. Add in the melted butter and process for another minute.

Press the cookie mixture into a 9-inch pie pan, making sure to come up the sides and completely cover the bottom.

Chill the crust for 1 hour.

Heat ½ cup of the cream with the cracked coffee beans in a small saucepan until bubbles form around the edges. Remove the pan from heat and strain the beans out of the cream.

Pour the warm cream over the chocolate and let it sit 2–3 minutes, then stir until the chocolate is completely melted into the cream. Let this mixture cool until almost room temperature.

Beat the remaining 1½ cups cream until soft peaks form. Pour in the cooled chocolate mixture, whiskey, vanilla, and salt. Beat again for another 2–3 minutes until the cream is thickened and the chocolate is fully incorporated.

Spread the mousse into the pie crust. Chill 2–3 hours before serving.

Fudgy Cocoa Brownies

Makes 16 brownies

Besides a classic chocolate chip cookie recipe, a perfectly fudgy brownie recipe is probably one of the most important to have on hand. You never know when you're going to want brownies, but it happens all the time. This recipe makes my favorite kind of brownies—super rich, dense, fudgy squares. I'm not a fan of cakey brownies and we never use frosting or icing on ours. They should have a crackly crust, not icing! I save my icing for cake. These are great on their own and they make a delicious base under a scoop of ice cream.

10 tablespoons butter
1 cup + 2 tablespoons sugar
¾ cup + 2 tablespoons unsweetened cocoa
    powder
¼ teaspoon salt

1 teaspoon vanilla extract
2 tablespoons brewed coffee, cooled
2 teaspoons instant espresso
2 eggs
½ cup all-purpose flour

Preheat the oven to 325°F. Line the bottom and sides of an 8 x 8 pan with parchment paper or foil.

Either over a double boiler or in a microwave-safe dish, mix the butter, sugar, cocoa, and salt and heat until the butter is melted and the mixture is smooth. Let the mixture cool until it's just slightly warm—it will look gritty right now, but that's okay!

Stir in the vanilla, brewed coffee, and instant espresso.

Add in the eggs, one at a time, stirring after each one, making sure the eggs are completely blended into the batter.

Stir in the flour, mixing until it is completely incorporated. Stir for another 30–40 strokes.

Spread into the pan and bake at 325°F for 30–35 minutes or until a toothpick comes out clean.

Let the brownies cool almost completely before slicing.

ACKNOWLEDGMENTS

Thank you to my family, above all, for believing in me and supporting my every endeavor.

Thank you to Nicole Frail, my editor, who answered endless questions, provided unending support and encouragement, and helped me make this book the best it could be.

And the biggest thanks is to my husband, Nick. Through the months of writing this book, you never questioned the time I was spending cooking, tasting, and typing. Thank you for being my trusty taste-tester and partner in coffee-drinking crime.

INDEX

Smoky black bean soup, 107
Smoky coffee marinated pork chops, 103
Spiced chocolate, 45
Spiced cinnamon rolls with coffee glaze, 24
Spiced coffee marinade, 81
Spiced grilled steak tacos, 99
Spiced whipped cream, 79
Spicy roasted potatoes, 109
Strawberry chocolate chiller, 59
Sweet and salty ice cream topping, 73
Sweet and spicy beef, 101

T
Triple chip espresso cookies, 119

V
Vanilla
    coffee vanilla banana bread, 23
    espresso vanilla chip scones with vanilla
        espresso glaze, 39
    Java vanilla fruit dip, 71
    multigrain waffles with vanilla maple glaze,
        19
    vanilla bean, 47
    vanilla bean smoothie, 56
    vanilla maple glaze, 19, 84

W
Waffles with vanilla maple glaze, 19

CONVERSION CHARTS

METRIC AND IMPERIAL CONVERSIONS

(These conversions are rounded for convenience)

Ingredient	Cups/Tablespoons/Teaspoons	Ounces	Grams/Milliliters
Butter	1 cup=16 tablespoons= 2 sticks	8 ounces	230 grams
Cream cheese	1 tablespoon	0.5 ounce	14.5 grams
Cheese, shredded	1 cup	4 ounces	110 grams
Cornstarch	1 tablespoon	0.3 ounce	8 grams
Flour, all-purpose	1 cup/1 tablespoon	4.5 ounces/0.3 ounce	125 grams/8 grams
Flour, whole wheat	1 cup	4 ounces	120 grams
Fruit, dried	1 cup	4 ounces	120 grams
Fruits or veggies, chopped	1 cup	5 to 7 ounces	145 to 200 grams
Fruits or veggies, puréed	1 cup	8.5 ounces	245 grams
Honey, maple syrup, or corn syrup	1 tablespoon	.75 ounce	20 grams
Liquids: cream, milk, water, or juice	1 cup	8 fluid ounces	240 milliliters
Oats	1 cup	5.5 ounces	150 grams
Salt	1 teaspoon	0.2 ounces	6 grams
Spices: cinnamon, cloves, ginger, or nutmeg (ground)	1 teaspoon	0.2 ounce	5 milliliters
Sugar, brown, firmly packed	1 cup	7 ounces	200 grams
Sugar, white	1 cup/1 tablespoon	7 ounces/0.5 ounce	200 grams/12.5 grams
Vanilla extract	1 teaspoon	0.2 ounce	4 grams

OVEN TEMPERATURES

Fahrenheit	Celcius	Gas Mark
225°	110°	¼
250°	120°	½
275°	140°	1
300°	150°	2
325°	160°	3
350°	180°	4
375°	190°	5
400°	200°	6
425°	220°	7
450°	230°	8